GLASS
CABIN

©2024 Tina Mozelle Braziel and James Braziel

ISBN 979-8-9874076-7-7

Published by Pulley Press, an imprint of
Clyde Hill Publishing

Book design and illustrations by Dan D Shafer
Cover art by Dylan Braziel
Photos courtesy Tina Mozelle Braziel and James Braziel

PULLEY
PRESS

GLASS
CABIN

TINA MOZELLE BRAZIEL

JAMES BRAZIEL

CONTENTS

INTRODUCTION

ON THE ART OF SEEING IN AND SEEING OUT:
Tina Mozelle Braziel and
James Braziel's *Glass Cabin*

> *"I think hard times are coming, when we will be wanting the*
> *voices of writers who can see alternatives to how we live*
> *now, and can see through our fear-stricken society and its*
> *obsessive technologies, to other ways of being."*
> —URSULA K. LE GUIN

TO BUILD A HOUSE OF GLASS, a person enters a
contract with reality. No matter where the inhabitants stand,
they see out—out to the coyote and the dandelion, the cedar
weed and the garden clearing. They see that the tree needs
the bird and the bird needs the worm and the worm needs the
human. The fact of a window teaches us that, although the
human enjoys the illusion of shelter, of being guarded and
apart, we are not.

Tina Mozelle Braziel and James Braziel built a house of glass
on an unwanted ridge in Alabama. Ten acres, $6000, and a
desire to no longer define their time as money. In *Glass
Cabin*, they have given us a record book, an almanac of
building their house, their love, their marriage. As a guide,
this book ostensibly teaches us how to survive by our own

strong hands. And what more important guide could there be, in this time of climate change and structural upheaval?

I'll tell you. It is this book's remarkable revelations about interdependence that makes it a work of art, both beautiful and needed. Much like their house, this book is built—at every joint and beam—in a structure of collaboration. Here is a guide for how to surrender to a love for all living beings, a love that radically transforms our understanding of the word *self*, the word *profit*, of the word *wealth*.

The minutes, hours, and days of our lives were not always counted by a factory clock. Remembering that in this present moment, in which most of us wake up winding a kind of factory clock inside our own anxious and austerity-terrorized minds, requires a courageous imagination. Ursula K. Le Guin mapped this truth when she accepted her Medal for Distinguished Contribution to American Letters: "We live in capitalism. Its power seems inescapable; so did the divine right of kings. ...Power can be resisted and changed by human beings; resistance and change often begin in art, and very often in our art—the art of words."

Dear reader, in your hands you hold a work of such courage, written by two love birds who just couldn't help themselves but fall for what is greater than the self. I hope you will keep it by your bedside and read a new page every tired morning. I hope you will leave it open in your cubicle and read a poem when your eyes hurt too much to look again at that addicting screen. And I hope you will go home at night and walk outside and see that the stars, the light that died to make you, are your stars, and you are theirs, and that this belonging is your only job. Le Guin continued on to say, "The name of our beautiful reward is not profit. Its name is freedom." Dear reader, in your hand you hold the hard-won good news that freedom is not just your reward, it is your birthright. *Glass Cabin* is a true work of art; it is a work of the truest art I know.

— REBECCA GAYLE HOWELL

for Hydrangea Ridge

PREFACE

WEEKENDS IN SPRING 2011, I drove out, divining like old timers witching for water. Only I was witching for a place to build a home. An acre or two, that's all I needed, and more importantly, what I could afford.

I jotted down numbers handwritten on sale signs. I stopped at convenience stores and BBQ joints, asked cashiers and the people waiting in line if they knew where I could get land. The Great Recession had ended but it didn't feel like it. As the owner of Benedikt's Restaurant put it when we spoke, "Everyone needs money now."

I had moved to Birmingham, Alabama, back in the fall to teach. Nobody gets rich teaching, but the job does come with a steady paycheck. Important because I brought Dylan, my youngest, with me. Wouldn't be easy—a new high school his senior year—but I'd been a stay-at-home dad and always taken care of him and his sisters, and his mother and I were heading for a divorce.

The fresh start had me dreaming about what I wanted, which was a writing life, which meant living somewhere that inspired and just having day after day to put down words.

Problem was the apartment rent. Took almost half my paycheck, and that one expense alone made it hard to keep

up with the other bills. A writing life seemed impossible.
If I could get some land, build a simple box, something
permanent—not mortgaged or rented—maybe then, I told
myself, I could have it.

Where I went was rural, where people not so well-off lived,
places and people that reminded me of the South Georgia
community I grew up in. By the end of summer, the Alabama
plateaus and bluffs and creeks and mountain pines had become
part of my blood, for I'd made the full compass, spoke
by county road spoke. B town—my affectionate name for
Birmingham because Atlanta has always been the A side of this
Southern record—was my hub.

But none of my divining got me a place until Bob Harvey gave
me a call. Bob's a real estate agent who pointed on a map in
his office in April to what he called Wild Land. "Nobody wants
that land now," he said then. "But you, it's what you want."

A developer had gone belly-up in the 2008 housing crash. His
dream—turn the woods around Sally Branch, a stream running
into the Blackburn Fork of the Little Warrior River, into
a suburbia heaven. Problem was water. The small town below
didn't have the money to pipe water uphill to heaven. And
the developer didn't either. Digging a well for a single
homestead meant churning 300, 400, as much as 700 feet
through chert, which took a lot of patience, pipe, and money.
I figured I could get around that by catching water free
from the sky.

After I talked with Bob, a bad night of tornadoes swept in
from Mississippi. "Once in a generation" is what the weather
authority said about the loss of property and people. I
wrote an op-ed for the *New York Times* about a devastated
neighborhood, Pratt City. This is some of what I witnessed—

Whole buildings gone. One entire neighborhood off
Avenue W gone. Around us are piles of wood and so
much wire—thick cables draped over dented cars,
wrapped into lassos on street corners. We see tar paper
trapped in chain-link fences, smell gas seeping from
broken pipes. Tin and plastic hang on to the last ends
of branches of fallen oaks and sycamores, full of paper
but stripped of leaves. A girl lies atop a set of bureau
drawers in the center of the rubble. She fidgets, tries
to sleep, her presence telling us that even in all this
destruction, some things are left whole.

It was my first introduction to the apocalyptic nature of
Alabama, and it had me questioning if I should even build
a home.

That was April. August now.

"You still interested in those ten acres?" Bob Harvey said
on the phone in a voice made rough by his age. Really, the
question wasn't a question—despite my worries, I was.
"They've decided to accept your offer."

A bank had purchased the wood lot at auction for next to
nothing, and told Bob Harvey to get rid of it when land
prices stayed low. I offered $6,000 in June. They countered
with $20,000. In July, they went down to 10. Then they took
me up on my 6.

Hydrangea Ridge is what I renamed Bob's Wild Land after the
leggy oakleaf hydrangeas that nudge their way out from under
the canopy of trash trees. Clearcut in the 90s, the soil
simply took root from whatever would grow—hickory and wild
cherry, poplar and sumac and sourwood, dogwood, cedar, silver
maple and red maple, all types of oak and pine. The ground

cover is more huckleberry bush than anything else—they make
a deliciously sour berry—and the acres cover a steep ridge
that washes to Sally.

Dylan said he would help build the cabin I wanted. Madi, my
middle daughter, said she could help during breaks from
college. My oldest, Jessi, had taken a new job in Cincy
that took all her time. Sorry that she couldn't get down
to Alabama, she sent encouragement instead. My pop said he
would get started on the design—he'd drawn a blueprint in
the 60s and from it, built a home for his family. And there
was Tina.

I fell in love with her at the 280 Boogie where we danced
to band after band all afternoon. In fact, we boogied so
long, my calves were sore for a week. My body's still trying
to catch the sway of her hips, which starts in her stomping
shoes and ends in her river hair. Tina knows how to turn a
dress, and I'm crazy about her.

That summer we stepped and counter-stepped. I even took her
dancing on the Easley Covered Bridge where we picnicked on
arugula and chevre and tomato sandwiches she made. So hot,
the tin roof popped. I sweated spinning her through the
creosote air.

When she left for Oregon in the fall with her belongings
to study poetry, I promised her a home when she returned,
though I doubted she would give up real mountains, hot
springs, the Pacific, and vineyards for what I could offer.
"Won't be an easy life out here," I said.

She said, "I grew up in a trailer park. I worked as a
counselor for delinquent boys and helped them build temporary
homes in the woods. I know how to make do. And I know how
to do without." I didn't ask if she saw me as delinquent.

Tina helped with the build on her winter and summer breaks, and two years later, she arrived at my apartment with our marriage license and her degree in hand, the cabin far from done. What we had—a foundation made of posts, a subfloor, studs for walls, a sloped roof. So we hustled, the work breathless that June, July, and August, leaving us eaten up by chiggers and sweat, exhausted.

On Labor Day, with the apartment lease up, Dylan moved into his new rental. Tina and I headed just north of B town and woke up in a tent on our subfloor. We hammered in frames for glass all fall while thunderstorms flashed the nights open, wet and blue. Mosquitoes, spicebush butterflies, walking sticks, and squawking Carolina wrens treated the cabin like a bridge from one side of the woods to the other. One morning a curious deer stepped through the doorless doorway—the nature outside had claimed us.

We took showers at the local gym. We got a woodstove, a 1970s Vestal. We took the backseat out of Tina's van and made it into a sofa. "Luxury camping," she called our way of living because Tina knows how to find good in the difficult.

We got dried-in by winter, but since then, the work has gone slow—our hands are the labor we can afford. Who knew building a cabin would become a way of life?

Imagine a glass cabin standing atop a grid of wooden posts just down from the crest of a ridge, swallowed up by trees and birds and snakes and the mist that comes off a branch bed. Imagine labor intertwined with nature, intertwined with dancing, routine, and love. That's us.

And I have the writing life I wanted, though Tina insists ours is a creative life. "Everything we do here," she says, "is a creative act. Don't you see that?" As usual, she is right. ◣

THE ACHE
WON'T QUIT

Dandelion

TINA

My first trip, I scoured every floor
of the MoMA, winding around other patrons
before they could read "Alabama" on my tee.
I lingered before "The Birthday," snagged
by its lovers levitating into kiss.
Then I moved as if driven, until I found,
unreal and gleaming, an Airstream. I made myself
at home. I took a seat. I cranked the slatted glass
open and peered out at the nearby Eames
and Starck. You'd think I had never seen
metal rivets before. I had never seen anything
from where I come from hailed as art. I want that
trailer-inside-the-MoMA feeling again now, I want
dandelion seed valued as much as tulip bulbs.
So I'm buying this packet of what most want
to poison. And the dream of putting down
roots. It has nothing to do with dandelions
that sprout and blossom into suns and moons
as bright and mythic as any Chagall.
Or how their greens fill bowl and belly.
Or how my bees will ferment their nectar
into honey. That's all free and easy.
Those seeds I could harvest from any lawn.

> It's worth I'm after.
> And always paying for.

WHAT I KNOW of work and worth started in fifth grade, when the time clock clamped down and I jumped, feeling a tug on the card stock. I lifted it and ran my finger over the impression 6:28 a.m. left before I slipped the card in a slot with my mom's and my brother's, a slot marked with our last name.

Started with $3.35 an hour, my brother and I cleaning the clinic, where the doctor treated people without insurance and even if they hadn't paid their last bill. We dusted and straightened magazines in the waiting room that was filled with Naugahyde furniture patched with electrical tape. We carried trash to a plywood platform out back and scoured examining room sinks and restroom toilets. That was supposed to take up every minute Mom drove the school bus, picked up our classmates, then returned to pick us up. While we sat in our fourth and fifth grade classrooms, she worked at the clinic drawing blood. On Tuesdays and Thursdays, she drove thirty miles east to Anniston to earn a medical assistant certificate.

Started with how practiced me and my brother were at doing chores and how we hadn't learned how time becomes money. What mattered to us was clocking out, so we could slide down the metal banister that ran beside the gurney ramp and wage rubber band wars from the enormous supply we found in a cabinet. Peering into the rusty drawers of the 1950s examining tables and imagining bodily things plopping into them mattered to us. I had read *Cheaper by the Dozen* and felt inspired by the father's job as an efficiency expert. Figuring out the fastest way to do things mattered to me too.

Started with being told to watch D, a grandmother, whose third job was to sweep and mop. If she dozed leaning on a mop or slumping into the vibrating recliner stored in the back room, we should wake her. It wasn't right sleeping on the clock. Started with the first and only time I shook her arm.

Started with how small our first paychecks were, how Mom asked to see our timecards. How she sat us down to talk and explained that it was necessary to be thorough and to double-check our work even if it took longer. Every additional minute was necessary. Our family needed the money while she was in school. "Ask for more work if you get done quick," she said.

Started with asking the doctor and nurse who lived in the apartment attached to the clinic what else I could do. Started with folding mounds of clothes, filmy boxer shorts I'd never encountered before, and polishing row after row of nursing shoes laid out on an examining table. Somehow that time weighed more, took longer, than before.

Started when Dad asked, "How much time will it cost you?" when I told him I wanted to buy a Swatch Watch. To me, a Swatch was a good value because I would wear it every day forever. And it would make everything I wore cool: my cut-offs, dresses my grandmother made, and the culottes, which I spelled cool-lots because it meant lots of cool. To Dad, a Swatch was an overpriced bit of plastic.

"Take my broken lawn chair," he said. "The way I figure, I could buy a brand new one that's ready to go for three hours of laying steel while sweating through my jeans. Or for only 15 minutes of work I can buy a roll of webbing and spend 20 minutes reweaving the seat myself."

"Time," he warned, "is the real cost. Money is nothing but a middleman put there to fool you."

I didn't think his questioning how much it might cost fair. Dad made so much more than I did in an hour. He pointed out that I didn't pay rent for our trailer lot or a truck payment or insurance or power bills. He could and would have gone on, but I cut him off, knowing what I owed him.

I didn't buy a Swatch. My brother did. He saved up just enough for the smaller one. When his friends pointed out he was sporting a "girl" Swatch, he gave it to me. But it didn't make me or my outfits cool. It didn't "go" with everything. When I did wear it, I became time obsessed. I kept trying to fit in as much as possible before the hour was up. That made me anxious and often late, so I swore off wearing watches altogether.

Having time banded around my wrist cost me too much.

Started with learning to rock climb when I was fourteen and teaching it the next year at summer camp. It started with working the drive-thru at Burger King in high school and washing dishes at the Montevallo Grille in college. It started with leaving my job at an eco-travel company at a lakeside office in the woods because even that cost me too much time outdoors. It started with working as a Wilderness Counselor, building "tents" by draping tarps over pine frames with delinquent boys and staying in them, with the joke that I slept in the woods with delinquents for a living.

Started with wanting to write poetry the way I had read stacks of library books as a kid, in the car, in a tree, on our deck or pier, somewhere or anywhere where I could hear birds, see a lizard.

Started when I realized that maybe Dad and I, all of us really, began at the wrong end. How much does it cost to work more than 40 hours a week, often at two or three jobs, and make less than a living wage? How much life, how much well-being, how much potential? How much time should it cost to put a roof over your head? To feed yourself and the ones you love? ◣

Down at the Trespass

My brother plants jubilees in perfect rows. I hoe out beggar's lice and citrons, thin seedlings three feet apart. Come mid-June, his fields are broadleaf winding calf-high, the melons hidden and dull green ready.

Cutters cut stem from vine, pickers spin jubilees down the line to the road. The county farmers say, "Best to work two crews opposite ends 'cause snakes learned long ago to shift away from earth's vibrations."

Between the crews, snakes oxbow, their back and forth getting shorter, until trapped in the field's middle where the pickers kill them.

One afternoon, we finish picking a field early, and my brother drives Red to the PittStop to get everyone drinks. I'm in back with the wind blowing sand like fire ants off the rusting bed. At the curve, a diamondback is crossing.

My brother swerves to hit it, misses. He punches the brakes and Red tightens up, sends me rolling, thudding against the cab.

It was twelve years ago when two boys crossed the curve on a motorcycle. The Trans Am driver didn't brake. Caskets couldn't be opened for viewing. The county farmers say, "Not the driver's fault. A blind spot there."

My brother aims the wheels, jams the gears, the transmission whines in reverse. And the diamondback coils up on the double yellow line, rattling at me as if I'm its foe.

TWO

For the rest of summer I dream of sand, black widows under the
bellies of jubilees, dead curls and the dull green of ripe. I dream of
cantaloupes growing like the plated shells of gopher turtles—sixty
million years they been 'round. And though I don't believe in church,
when I find a gopher turtle, I lay hands because to know the world,
you have to feel it.

Some people put 'em on their back, watch 'em paw at earth out of
reach. I can't tell you how many gophers I find that way dead. Live in
a place half-wild, you see cruelty, our kind.

And you see our designs—

Box homes, single trailers multiplying into doublewides. Chicken
houses and barns built like churches. Field rows hitched to flat and
hitched to hill, everything split into property or rural electric.

And nature's designs—

The keyholes coyotes claw out of the ripest melons, needing to break
apart just one. The dugout gopher holes where rattlers shack up. And
the penny sheen of copperheads cooling on the sand at dusk.

People expect me to look them in the eye, but I keep watching the
ground for snakes. One time a man grabbed my chin, lifted my face.
"Up here," he said like I wasn't giving him respect enough. Some people,
I tell you, they got nerve.

As my brother runs over the diamondback again and again, it becomes stretched-out woozy, showing more white belly roll than diamond ridge.

My brother cuts its tail off—a prize of six rattles and a button—slips the hollow scales into a jelly jar lid to shake at my ear as a prank. He doesn't know I sneak into his room to hear the dead rattle in a silent house, the rev of Red passing over, the thunk of the diamondback striking the chassis beneath my knees and trembling hands.

MY HANDS HURT all the time now. I sleep with them
ready to strike nails with a hammer, push the bar of a
chainsaw through the dark rings of a tree. I get up—can't
sleep well like this—tell my hands "Relax," tell myself, "The
nails will get driven tomorrow. The firewood will get cut,
and we'll be warm through winter." Rest of the night I'm half-
dreaming under a moon our skylight shows as a bright nickel
in one corner, hours later as a dime above my feet. We've
been living in our glass cabin for over a decade, but the
ache won't quit.

It's something I share with Pop. He built his home as much as
he could with his own labor. My job? Plug/unplug the circular
saw after the on/off switch wore out. He preferred that saw
'cause it cut straight.

What money Pop made as a teacher, a cashier at the Colonial
Store, water meter reader for his hometown, and doing a
paper route on Sundays went into keeping his family fed—I'm
one of his four children—and into the farm. Legend in the
county has it, Pop barb-wired all two hundred acres himself—
posts dug, strands pulled. When I got old enough, I helped
with the mending since Pop's cows love to wreck fences for
the taste of grass on the other side. Nothing worse than
getting that call from the Sheriff at two a.m., a Brahman
heifer having hit the road and gotten slammed by a sleepy

driver. Keeping insurance was tricky. But Pop loves Brahmans for their humped backs and big ears. They love to wander.

In high school, I worked melon fields for the county farmers, so damn hot in June and July walking those rows. What I found there was this—Didn't matter my age or yours, didn't matter how much money my parents made or yours made or you made, black or brown or white skin didn't matter because the sun overtook all concerns. It blistered us all the same. Made us all thirsty. Length of a row mattered. Getting to a jug of water at the end of that row mattered. And us working together mattered—picking, tossing, stacking melons to be thrown later to a packer on the back of a truck who swaddled each melon with his hands and wrists, melons weighing twenty, thirty, forty pounds made of red water and black seed and sugar. The packer set them on a bed of hay into a perfect green pyramid for market.

I never understood when I stepped outside those fields the hate of every color of skin that wasn't white. Stopping in town to get gas or supplies meant stepping through the remnants of slavery-confederacy-jim crow in jokes and comments and rebel flag decals. Hate was always on a low boil, waiting to boil over.

And the quick blame in conversations assigned to people for what they didn't have. "If they were just smarter, if they worked harder, if they, if they—" is what the ones who had some ease because they had some money said about those who didn't. What I found in these prejudices was a disregard, a discounting, a way to not know a person.

But down the rows there was something about the willingness to do what was not easy. Something about the time spent laughing as a way of shrugging off the sun. Something about just spending time and getting paid cash at the end of the day made a bond.

Pop still mends fences. A Great Depression baby, he's in his 90s. I help him when I'm down in South Georgia. Work not yet done is the same for us, an ache we can't sleep away. Back in those melon fields in June and July, I couldn't get the sand out of my sleep.

Sometimes now that same grit shows up with a nickel moon and restlessness. Sometimes the people I knew in the rows appear with hands rubbed smooth by field dirt to lift and carry me through the heat. Sometimes I carry them. ◣

A SIMPLE BOX

POP PLAYED THE CALL to worship one Sunday, "Bringing down the roof!" as he likes to say, then the preacher got up to preach. First, she mentioned the glass to the congregation. Tempered, the panes had protected the stained glass of the church for years, but the barbeque chicken fundraiser on Saturday made enough money to replace it with plexi. She pointed at the glass. "If any of you want it before it goes to the dump, let me know."

Pop raised his hand. ◣

Making Church Glass Ours

TINA

To scrape the church off, we spent Christmas break
laying panes across sawhorses in Pop's yard,
taking razor blades and Goo Gone to silicone

gone dark with mildew, scraping away what sealed
them to stained glass. We saved Pop's palmprint
from the Sunday he raised his hand to claim

church panes for us by not scouring
how Dad taught, wiping away fingerprints
until panes are nothing to see but through.

But we cleaned like we would any rented house
claiming with a scrubbing that says there's no clean
like mine. Bundling them up in rags, side by side

in my van, we made ourselves forget how glass is
liquid stilled, a lake where one comes to sip,
to see themselves, to slip inside. We hauled them

home, down 300 backroad miles, reaching back
to lay on hands as we eased over train tracks,
waited out thunderstorms. All to keep each pane

upright, innocent of shatter. We left our panes
leaning on tulip poplars out of the wind, away
from the drip of pine until we could frame them

into walls. The rest lean on trees still,
look out at the ridge, mirroring its prayer.

WHEN WE VISITED Samuel Mockbee's Rural Studio in Hale County, I left thinking, *I can do what they're doing*, even though I had never built a house before. There, architecture students from Auburn University design and build homes for those who don't have much. Beautiful, inexpensive simple boxes made in part from secondhand materials—old license plates turned into shingles, waxed-corrugated cardboard bales stacked into walls, car windshields a pavilion roof. But first, I had to clear the land. ◣

How To Make a Clearing

WHAT YOU'LL NEED FOR THIS PROJECT

3 Red Flags

1 Measuring Tape

1 Chainsaw

1 Can of Gas/Oil Mixture

1 Pint Bar-and-Chain Oil

1 Round File with Guide

2 Bottles of Water

2 Pairs of Gloves

100 feet into the woods, find the hydrangea Tina marked as the northeast corner of the cabin. She's in Oregon now, giving poetry her tune. But Dylan's here. Give him the good **gloves** and have him reel out 30 feet of **measuring tape** south.

Have him stick 1 **red flag** into the ground. Then reel 30 feet west, **red flag**. 30 feet north, **red flag**. Those flags and that hydrangea mark the 4 corners.

Last time you were down helping Pop mend fences, he paid you with a **chainsaw**. Pick it up. Pull the rope. WARNING: Chainsaws are finicky. You can wear an arm out trying to crank one.

But once you do, squeeze the throttle trigger and tell Dylan to get out of the way. Watch for a pine's lean, then notch the pine's belly. Watch sawdust fly.

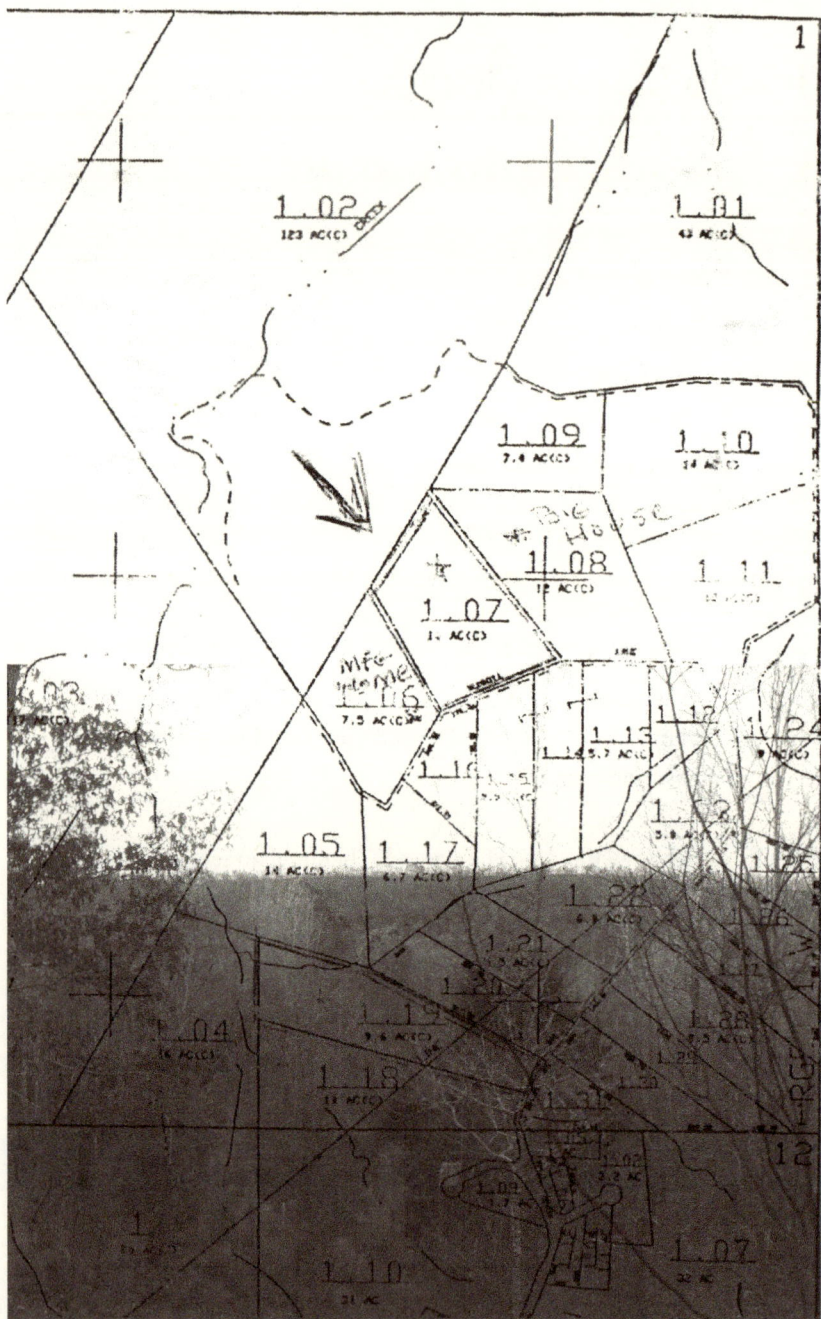

1

1.02
123 AC(C)

1.01
43 AC(C)

1.09
7.4 AC(C)

1.10
14 AC(C)

BIG HOUSE

1.08
12 AC(C)

1.11
12 AC(C)

1.07
1. AC(C)

1.03

M fe
Home
1.06
7.5 AC(C)

1.13
5.7 AC(C)

1.12

1.24

1.16

1.22
3.9 AC

1.05
18 AC(C)

1.17
6.7 AC(C)

1.25

1.20
6.3 AC(C)

1.21

1.23
3.5 AC

1.04
16 AC(C)

1.19
9.6 AC(C)

1.18
11 AC(C)

1.31

1.02
3.2 AC

1.09

1.07
32 AC

1.10
21 AC

12

SEE MAP 29-03

Kick the notch out. Make a felling cut from the back. If lucky, the pine snap-falls to the dirt, but more than likely, it gets hung-up in its neighbors' branches.

Try to push the pine bole to the ground. If that doesn't work, and it probably won't, STOP. Take time to figure this out because pressure points you see along the bark's bowing and bending may not be in the grain.

WARNING: Trees roll, pin, injure, kill, and boles that move like bears determine your luck, good or bad.

Once, something inside a storm-blown chinaberry snapped, and my brother's saw kicked, and the chain, still turning, turned through his wrist. He wrapped his shirt 'round the wound, drove home from the barn where our mother shrieked like a hawk, driving him to the hospital. They stitched him, he was fine, his veins untouched.

Seamus Heaney said—"The way we are living, timorous or bold, will have been our life," so slice into the hanging trunk from the top 'cause you can't afford to hire your worries out. When the sapwood starts to close up the wound, let off the trigger, and remove the bar before the pinch.

Make a final cut from underneath. When the pine slips back, spin out of its way. TIP: Take a couple of dancing lessons before first-time chainsaw use. The Perrodin Two Step is particularly helpful here.

Push the rest of the tree to the ground.

Know that pines gum up chimneys. Poplars burn too quick to make coals. So cut and haul them beyond the red flag corners to rot. But saw oak, maple, hickory, dogwood, and wild cherry into 2 foot lengths for Dylan to stack for your first winter.

Be careful. Stumps trip. Sharpen chain as needed. Refill reservoirs. Use. Common. Sense.

When Dylan says, "I'll miss you when you're out here," tell him you love him because it's true. But don't tell him it will do no good if the two of you keep living in the same house. Don't tell him, he has to grow up to survive. Don't tell him you want and need your own life. Not yet, not ever. Just get him to where he needs to be.

When done, rest on an oak stump. A square of blue will be above you. Take off the **gloves**. Drink plenty of **water**. Let the sun warm you from the cold, and wonder about the woods, how they feel about the sudden absence of trees and your presence. Temporary, the way things are.

Texts

TINA: I love how you open your arms gate-wide
so I can lie on the field of you, how you close
them around my shoulders, how quick you open
them so I can kiss you. I love how far you reach,
laying word next to word, building a bridge
from Hydrangea Ridge to the Willamette River,
a bridge that your love crosses, 2400 miles
traversed in moments.

JIM: I love watching your hands, what they do,
how they curl like red oak leaves, how they split
water, how they open sun. I wish I could be the
cup you wrap your hands around each morning
after you've been dreaming, the hot coffee
swirling, making you warm, or the glass of juice,
cold orange making your fingers shiver and
wiggle. And the fork, the spoon. I love holding
your hands, swinging them into dance. I could
walk forever that way. I love how you cross your
hands in your lap, rest them, rest them in mine,
how you rub down your skirts and a dog's coat,
how your knuckles jump as you knit. I love how
you curl your hand under your chin, how you set
your hands to my face. How my fingers always
seek yours to intertwine, to trace back what your
hands did all day, all the things you touched and
gripped and moved and cared for.

TINA: Each morning, some afternoons, at bedtime, I read your texts, feel that bridge holding me, letting me cross the Great Divide back to you. How you span space and time so even now we are together.

Sun-Drenched

TINA

Please dream me lying
on the sun-drenched boards
of a pier, goose-pimpling
from wind, feeling sun kiss
away the damp like you do.
I'll conjure you to me. Did I
tell you I love how piers look
like bridges going nowhere?
Isn't that what our love is?
A place we spread quilt, carry
cooler, see sky as ceiling,
a nowhere place we make ourselves
a home. No need for another
shore when all is here, your eyes
shifting from one shade of water
to another, your curls flaring
in the breeze, your lips pursing
into mmmmhmm. Oh, how you send me
swimming between sun and water,
unafraid to rise, fall, find
harbor in your open chest.

Alchemies

Dylan lifts the posthole diggers, brings up a thin slip of red powder.
"You'll need a rock bar to get through that," is what Jim Owens told
me last week. He's from here and knows Alabama dirt, how it turns to
cement in a drought.

So I throw the six foot iron bar in like a javelin. I do this over and over,
but the ground keeps slipping through the jaws of the diggers.

"Let me get water," Pop says, his alchemy for turning dust to mud.
Sixteen holes—that's how many we have to dig, and this is the first
one.

Dylan hits the root of a pine but can't cut through, so I spear the earth
until chunks of root tear free and the smell of rosin lifts with the dust
and he can go on working.

The sky grumbles, flares all the way from Locust Fork. Maybe the ten
percent chance the weatherman's been preaching will fall in our favor.
Maybe the lightning and wind and turkey vultures will shift the sky
with their promise.

Back from his truck, Pop pours water from a milk jug. "Now try it," he
says. New mud sticks to the jaws when Dylan brings up the handles.
Still so many things to tell him, to show him, to let him learn.

When he gets tired, I take over, my chest carrying fire down the center
where rock bar throwing has shaken up bone and muscle.

"Don't have a stroke," Pop says. "Not worth it."

I say, "I'm too young," loud enough to hope that's true, but all I want is Tina—she gives me a calm I don't have.

We're down three feet. Pop notches four on a handle with the scratch of a nail. Sun gets so weak it leaves us.

I throw the rock bar in like a javelin, and it sparks bright against chert Tina would call pretty. Her grandparents were rockhounds who taught her to look for sparkle.

The cool of the earth comes up dark followed by my loud breath-catching soaked in sweat of this evening's song. Dylan's turn until "Got it," he says, the handles in the earth all the way to the scratch, and the dirt trapped in our hands and hair slips into our lungs.

Turkey vultures leave to follow the drafts. Lightning strikes northwest over Allgood now, suppertime, and our drought not yet broken.

Everlast JIM

Think of ice. Cool water. The way people call ice tea "Nice Tea" here. Try to think winter.

My hands and wrists stay numb from spearing rock bars like javelins through claychertloam, numb as dead-handled wood and steel. Sweat burned my eyes a few days ago. Now, the salt in me has gone.

A sign I won't survive the apocalypse they taught you in church and you still believe is coming. But I have become more body than mind like I wanted.

Accept me this way, my love, all sweat digging four foot holes in the earth, wanting to believe in "Just keep going," even though it's getting harder to tell that lie.

And when you come home to me, I will ease the ache of your walking like you did for the women at your church, bending over a basin of water to wash their feet still encased in stockings.

46

Hive Step

Like a bee studying
        the waggle of her scout,
I read your step and turn,
        how you make me twirl.
Your moves give length,
        width, depth of what could be
made home. Even our first dance
        I took your measure
as true, an exact fit for you,
        for me, for all
the honey we're bound to brew.

What I Mean When I Say Help Like Hep

isn't "hep" as in hepcat, 1950s hip. No,
I'm mimicking the '80s Shake 'N Bake commercial
featuring a tiny girl proudly declaring,
"And I hepped," meaning the way I "helped"
Jim put in foundation posts by steadying
a power pole that I could not carry
or catch. But it stayed upright.
My laying hands on it was miracle.

And saying "hep" pays homage to Mam-maw
(said Mam Maw), who always said hep
and loaded sentences with triple negatives
like, "He ain't got no money, nohow"
and aiming them true as her pistol,
out shooting Pap-Paw two out of three
every target practice. And an homage to Mama,
who dropped so many l's one Thanksgiving,
my boyfriend heard her worries over rolls
(two parts self-rising flour, one part butter,
one part sour cream) as, "I toad you,
don't let my rose get code."

He poked fun at her so bad that when I learned
in my History of the English Language course
that centuries ago English speakers stopped
pronouncing the "l" in "should" and "would"
and that this phenomenon will happen again,
I told him, Mama's ahead of her time
instead of backward. It figures my people
would take such too far. But the way I see it,
that boyfriend damned well shouldn't.

Times I say "it don't" or "she don't"
takes me to Mam-maw spreading quilts
in the grass outside her trailer
so she could sit and watch us grandkids
hoot and holler, hurtling over her
rose bushes like track stars. I mean no
disagreement, no appropriation talking
like this, I mean I feel at home.

Still I get why I got the side-eye
at the airport for listening too close
to Black women talking to each other
in a way they won't talk to me
or other white people. They sound
more like family than anybody else.
Even their turning shoulders has me
wanting to call out the way Mam-Maw
said good-bye, "Need me, just holler."

Woodhenge

When I was a kid, light could barely get through the pines, their
perfect rows the quietest place for walking through, as if quiet hid
there, brown straw thick and smothering on the ground.

A panther tracked me once, moving trunk to trunk, for I'd seen
panther tracks in the Shell's field in the washed up sand at the low,
prints too wide to be a bobcat. This was before the clearcut, this place
of ghosts called old Minnie Lennard's Place and a portal between
Pop's fields and the true woods of the Alapaha, where, back in the 50s,
someone shot a bear near the river, the last the county has seen.

TWO

Now I walk the square of sixteen posts we set in imperfect rows over
summer, a foundation of dead trees ready to carry our glass cabin in
their crowns.

I still see you out here, my love, that day you wore railroad overalls,
ready to dig earth in the heat, quiet like you are, wanting to prove
your worth. But first, you reached an arm in, lifted rusty toads out of
the holes they had jumped into overnight.

Later, I said to rest when you got tired. I said, "It's okay," when you got
thirsty and gave you water. I said, "I've got you," as if I could catch you
like a tree falling. Jagged and in different lengths, soon I'll saw these
posts level, make them sumac in their height.

But walking like this, seeing you digging, I won't be doing this any longer. We build toward the sky, we lose what's underneath and still we want to be true, want our cabin to be the lookout for black bears and panthers returning.

Hummingbird

When I propped my feet
      on the porch rail this summer
and my red toenails attracted
      that hummingbird,
his feathers gleamed emerald
      as he hovered close,
ardent in his pursuit of succor.

      He turned his heart-colored throat
to me when I raised a glass
      of tea and proposed,
"This is all I offer, sugar
      steeped this dark, this cool."
You told me then there is more
      honey if I wanted to know.
"Not now," I said, "not now."

Walking to class, I call
      my feet flowers, count each toe
as petal. If I plucked them
      each foot would mean "you love me."

Don't you see, my love,
      how now I want more?
Not just honey you mix in tea,
      but you as hummingbird,
stirring me to brew
      nectar and blossom wide.

The Subfloor Blues JIM

Brought up on Logan Martin Lake, you love water. If you could, you'd
swim instead of walk. I've promised you more than once, I'll build you
a river so that lake of yours can at last be undammed.

After setting down plywood over joists, I set down a blue tarp to
protect the subfloor from rain I keep waking to, intermittent without
end, our drought finally broken. The water that pools, Dylan and I
sweep off before we can work.

December, your semester over, and you here with me for a while, so
I show you this lake I've made by accident, too cold to swim in, the
water too shallow, but something about the blue color of the tarp
makes me believe there's more depth here if only we were brave
enough to dive.

And you and your quiet? You're thinking—*This subfloor lake is crazy
business.* Or—*This is love. This is home.*

Rivering

Give me that broom,
      and I'll river,
sweep rain off
      our floor, swish it
around wall plates
      to waterfall
from our threshold.
      Watch me make this
pool stream down
      the ridge to Sally.

Help me right all
      I got wrong. That
this tarp would keep
      rain off without
slope enough to fall.
      Tell me all you want
is love, for me
      to say more, that
you'll take things
      I suggest the way
you pull peanuts,
      shaking off dirt,
giving water, heat,
      salt and more salt
until they taste
      just right.

Meander

Down here, a drizzle is called spit.
      Down here, rain rasps
gullies, cuts ruts, makes us
      pull the car over
because it sure sounds like hail
      and there's no seeing
the road for the ditch.

Down here, signs say go to church
      or the devil will get you,
though he's so gone on fiddling
      in Georgia, we can risk Sunday.
Down here, a water tower is made
      into a peach, and rivers
meander to the Gulf.

Down here, stars and bars
      soil so much even the sky
is stained. Down here is humid
      as it sounds: down in the swamp,
down in the cellar, down and out,
      the down here place we pat
a bit shyly between legs
      just before they open.

Strike It

your tongue is a map / of desert, and suddenly there's just
the noose and you, / darkness rolling out in all directions,
/ the stinging of so much quiet
—ASHLEY M. JONES

Ashley, on MLK day, around the curve that leads to Tina and me, I
saw a noose hung from a pine branch. This was some years ago before
we moved in. And the folks who did it are gone, got arrested. Not for
the noose. The police found stolen safes in their living room beside a
railroad spike and hammer. When I told a neighbor this story, she said,
"Give me the stars and bars over a noose any day." Rebel flags catch
every breeze in the county.

First thing, I slowed down to be sure. When I couldn't deny the rope
any longer, I sped up. *Go tear it down*, I thought, but if I did, that
neighbor could do damage to my home, could put someone I love in
peril. Though the noose puts you in peril, Ashley, and you are someone
I love. I did not know them, had never seen them out in their yard. I
should've knocked on the door and talked about it, but I don't have
faith in such words. I kept thinking, I'm the passerby while their
trailer holds a corner of these woods.

Ashley, the morning was stuck in a thick dew like the noose was
turpentine off the pine, like it was fifty years ago, and I was still in
South Georgia where racism swirled in every conversation as easy as
saying and lying, "I'm good, how you?" I'd learned to stay quiet in the
face of it, to take those voices in where they could do less damage. As if
words can be held down, the damage in.

How much longer will I keep a finger to my lips and say, "Shhh"? How much longer can I let the noose be? You would tell me, it's been too long already, Jim. You would tell me, one day the hammer hits the spike, breaks open the vault, and in our trembling, we sing.

Say Uncle

We say Uncle as if some bully twists our arms.
We say Uncle as in "family" who is not really
related, someone we suffer a seat at our table.
We say Uncle as in Uncle Sam, the one wanting
you and me, all of us.

We never name the grandfather who claimed the KKK
did good things too. We don't say how we answered
when he asked, "Don't you think punishing men
for beating women and children is good?"
A question so slippery it slopes.

Our neighbors shook their heads at the noose
someone hung in their yard for MLK day
years ago. We do nothing about the Confederate flag
waving day in and out just down the road. Odd
how much we want cake and to eat it too. Odd too
how we told Ashley about the noose, how we said
write it, work your magic, use threat as material.

Now Ashley reads her poem, points us out,
writers living in the midst of such. Everyone
turns, looks, and we say nothing, write nothing,
do nothing but whisper not us, not us,
but uncle, uncle, uncle.

I Married Him Before
He Got the Roof On

TINA

Married him before June,
before he said we're moving
        come September even if
we live in a tent.
        Married him before I saw
our ceiling was so high
        rain would blow in.
Married him before he tied
        an apron of nails
around my waist each morning.
        Before I learned measuring
twice and cutting once
        never guarantees getting it
right. Before I fathomed how
        this is more epic
than being benighted on a cliffside
        or backpacking slot canyons.
How nothing is left safe
        at home base. How I must carry
all that I have, all that I am,
        around saws and scaffolding,
through rainstorms and sawdust.
        Yes, I married him
before I got how all in
        all is. Married him
before he called me Trouble
        like he calls Dylan

and the cat, a pet he never wanted
      but now brushes, pours
a saucer of milk and cup of water.
      Before I knew he'd build
the cat a bed and line it
      with his own wool sweaters.
I married before I got the measure
      of a man is the trouble
he loves and how.

Sawzall Rhythm

— for Dylan —

Table saw, hacksaw, Japanese, jig. Pinch up the Sawzall with your left
hand, cradle the crosscut with your right. And don't forget the miter,
the circular, the bar-and-chain. For the gods made us many saws to cut
the world shorter.

Grab a hammer, the plumb bob, chalk line, chisel, the drill your hand
already feels the grip of. Hold the crushed boxes of nails and screws
tight so they can't spill—1 inch, 2 inch, 2 and 3/4, drywall black and
decking board tan, the ones labeled finishing, the #2 Phillips bit, the
T25 star.

Bring it all down the apartment stairs. Load it up in the Corolla Tina
calls a Tufted Titmouse. "Tough Titmouse," I say because that car's
really a truck. She holds 8' boards from gearshift to trunk.

Get in, swing the door close. We've got a 45 minute drive past the
flame of Tarrant, Jeff State, and the Super Bowl, just to get to
Hydrangea. Then dig everything out, haul it through the woods.

Plug in the table saw at the meter box Alabama Power left us. Plug in
the miter and crank up the country. We've gone through the R&B, the
old time rock, the news after news after news, and the Swap Shop.

"Country music is so damn proud," you say as we measure studs, cut
and glue, clamp, nail and screw together a 10' x 10' square. On three,
lift this wobble into balance, the first section of west wall, needing
glass to fill it.

"Let me get a picture of you framing sky," I say, and everything stops in the shutter-blink—radio station, wind rocking—I never framed the sky before. I don't understand why I waited.

You say, "Arms getting tired, Pop-pop," after being Atlas for such a long stretch. So we brace the wall while the wind spits rain. Our weather's chances leave only small stretches of dry to work in.

Pack up the god-saws, all the accoutrements. We've got 45 minutes to drive until we have to carry everything up the apartment stairs. Can't have anyone breaking into the Tough Titmouse and stealing what we must have tomorrow.

First thing, you go to your room to sleep. I charge the drill batteries, the smell of metal too deep in my skin to ever be washed out. Yes, there are more efficient ways to work, and people have gladly told them to me. But their ways of living and wanting is becoming less and less something I recognize as mine.

Texts

JIM: The exposed rafters are going up! Two foot
on center, they frame the sky in long rows of
blue sluices. If the rain holds off, they'll soon
frame our ceiling. Dylan and Jeff keep running
up the ladders like squirrels. Gravity has no say
over them.

What do you want to see when you wake up in
the loft? Rusted tin? Maybe I can get some in
South Georgia or you could ask on Facebook.

Or plywood like Ada and Dail's ceiling? There's
pretty plywood now. I saw one made of birch
at Lowe's.

Tongue and groove? Though that would be
expensive, and 2×4s are cheaper.

I love you and wish I were holding you rather
than holding on to rafters for dear life. Too much
gravity in me.

TINA: Wish I were there to see you frame sky. To
set my two feet on center. To become rafter you
cling to.

And pretty plywood? Does the birch hold the
dot-dash of its bark, morse code we can decipher
each night?

I just want to see you when I wake. I don't want
to sleep under a slow rain of rust from tin. I
think 2×4s will match our walls.

JIM: The plywood is not a dot-dot-dash bark
but shaved tree rings uncurled and glued flat.
Rains more sawdust than rust here. But there's a
sale—$2 for 2×4×8s. Pine, red with rosin. Boards
full of rivers that eddy around knots. When
sunlight hits them, they will be something to see,
your two feet set on center, holding me while I
carry you. I will build you a sky of red pine. 600
boards. Yes?

TINA: YES! Yes, to the red pine sky. Yes, to all
the wonder you build in and for me. Yes, to you
and me.

Honeymoon at Tor House

TINA

(Tor House, home and refuge built by Poet Robinson Jeffers)

Here, surf ignites the shore. Rock crags
into walls. And walls snug into house
and rally into tower. Here we learn
how Jeffers made stone love stone,

how Una Call took to tiny kitchen
and tower he built her. Like them,
we vow to mind our moorings, vow
to craft our home so it outcrops,

belongs there. Right now, our cabin
awaits a roof. Alabama rain sifts
through our rafters, washing down
a ridge more ancient than this

coastline and Saturn's rings.
But we are here, standing before
words Jeffers burned into his walls
vowing to do the same. We say look

at this joist, that sill, how Tor House
proves we can build our cabin
and still lay word beside word
like setting down granite, something

more forever than us. At the top
of the tower's keep, we stop silent,
mouths shaping a single syllable,
the awe a hawk polishes into sky.

It Will Happen

ONE

When I get too close to a paper nest in the eaves. When the wasps give
no buzzing warning. When their stings startle, send me and the ladder
I am climbing back to the dirt.

Every yellow jacket arrow I get on the ground, I record the bright ache
because if you get used to something, you control it.

TWO

The ladder falls on a loop.

Tina's father fell 50 feet when the rung he clutched broke. Everyone
thought he would die. I don't think Tina's ever accepted he made it.

And a woman I knew in Ohio, her husband fell off a ladder while
pruning a buckeye. She hated him but felt sorry for him, didn't think
she could divorce him now.

I tell myself not to death-grip the ladder in freefall. I tell myself in
the last second, "Jump away, roll," though this is not something I can
practice.

THREE

Or when I grab a tool under the cabin and disturb a rattler stretched
out from the heat, or coiled around a stick of wood in winter. Until the
snake moves, all those scales blend-in like jeweled leaves and metal.
Like wasps, it's not about menace. Every living thing here trains me to
give space, but training has limits.

FOUR

It did happen when Dylan and I put on the tin roof.

We tarpapered the ceiling boards, including the holes for the skylight and chimney. I drew those flimsy rectangles in red chalk, warning Dylan not to walk there.

May, 90 degrees hot, and I lost myself, walked right across the skylight, thinking about what? how the sun doesn't quit? about our honeymoon on the Big Sur, Tina snugged inside a sequoia smiling big as the trunk and my hand trying to reach her?

I fell through easy as air. I was falling, didn't have time to know I was. Caught hold a rafter.

"Don't die," Dylan said and grabbed my shirt and shoulder and did not let go until he fished me out.

"I'm sorry," was all I could say as we got our bearings and pulled tin up by ropes, untied the knots, set and sealed grooved edge over grooved edge.

We kept at it until we made tin rows into roof, then walked across eyelevel with the branches. For the first time I was burdenless, invincible as a hawk. Dangerous to believe that lie.

Texts

TINA: Southbound. I'm coming home
to you.

JIM: Come home, baby. I need
you and need your help.

Become Kindling

On the way to work, we pass the flame of Tarrant shooting out a steel pipe, its furnaces underneath distilling coal into coke. Been so dry, everything could become kindling.

My fingers tap the steering wheel like matchsticks. At Quick Motors, they staple Christmas lights to their billboard racecar so the wheels flicker.

Combustible semis line the loading dock at Shurfine Foods, and everywhere in Tarrant, smokestacks are flinging smoke, their clouds of benzene numbing our tongues.

The tall fiberglass man with forearms at forklift angles, he reaches out to gather the road in. GCR painted on his red shirt, he's got the devil's eyes. The flame of Tarrant jumps, he'll be the first to burn.

TWO

All day, we put arched glass in a wall that should've been finished weeks ago. And on the way back to our apartment, the flame of Tarrant shoots high through the dark. Pieces break off, head for the moon's paper craters, as the rest of the flame claws at what's lost, not wanting to lose more.

I should focus on the road—Tina and Dylan are asleep—but I keep slowing down, watching and waiting for the moon to catch. Makes the idea of building a cabin seem foolish. The act more urgent. I cannot tell you why I do this—shake Tina and Dylan, pull them from their dreaming, so their eyes will pool with fire.

A SIMPLE BOX — 69

Push

If I keep saying I love you will it be enough when I give you a hammer
and drill and ask you to brace these boards? I promised you a home by
summer but all I have to give is a roof and no dried-in walls.

The only cool we get is thunderstorms drawing heat out of the air
in their rush to get past. You won't live without AC—"That's non-
negotiable," you've said more than once, expecting repetition to make
words real.

I push that aside with the swelter—come September, we're out here no
matter what.

Right now all day every day is me pushing you and Dylan. "I love you,"
I say. I tell Dylan, "You won't be doing this much longer."

There's a place where we move past exhaustion, where our shoulders
become thick with work, and impossible to know if that will be shelter
enough when "keep going" is all that's left.

Right Now

the saw screams, spraying sawdust
down my shirt and into my bra
and I don't know what itches more
that or the sweat bees stinging
my elbows or the no-see-ums gnawing
my chin. Right now the sun glowers,
and our studs throw bars of shade.

Right now you're wrangling warped boards
with vise grips while a skink darts
over plywood flaunting his lightning
blue tail. Right now the roof is done
except for the skylight. Right now
the north wall is done except
we need a door hung. Right now

Dylan toenails another board in.
Right now I'm sweating through
my overalls and socks, dripping
silicone on the floor, bending more
nails than I dare count. Right now
Gatorade sweats on our only table,
High Life waits in the cooler. Right now

this board is cut too long. Right now
I'm going under the house to pee
in the bucket. Right now the saw trumpets,
the hammer drums. Right now birds go
silent while cicadas shake air

A SIMPLE BOX — 71

like a rattle. Right now humidity
lays a hand so heavy it will dunk
if not drown me. Right now

my knees creak as I get up. Right now
I'm taking a swallow of ice water
before I once again try cutting
this board back down to size.

After Work in the Last Week of July

JIM

The light comes through brilliant as if each tear in the clouded sky is a place for my hands to swim up and leave this carrying, setting heavy glass into frames. Last night I dreamed snow on the hilltop. The night before I dreamed of a yellow afternoon where trees had been planted and grown full of apples, chairs set next to them, and still no place for me to sit. Tomorrow I will set the day, get more done. Maybe sweat enough to make heat into cold, bring light into me.

Bending Tin

Dylan and I stand on ladders a few feet apart, putting pressure on
impact drivers, spinning screws so fast they spark-then-burrow into
the tin on the north wall.

Wears an arm out, so much pressure—but if an elbow drops, the
screws slip sideways, fall dumb to the earth, all that effort lost, and we
don't have time to retrieve them.

Dylan keeps looking at the sun to see how close it is to setting. He's got
plans for later. I keep listening for the partner of the timber rattler
I killed yesterday. It wandered a foot from where I was cooling off,
drinking water. When it gave warning, the still leaves moved.

I tell Dylan we're losing light, clouds coming in.

"We're losing light. We're losing light," he caws like a crow, laughing,
my tone too serious to take seriously, but I don't know how else to be.
Every afternoon, storms have turned the ridge into a river of twigs
and rocks and lost screws.

Then I get drawn in by a spinner, which I shouldn't—metal bits and
curls might flick into my eye. But the point breaks through, catches in
the wall stud, and I tighten down. I watch the next one and the next
one. Then I need Dylan's help to cut a seam for a window.

Gloved hands careful, he pulls sharp pieces away from the snips I'm
holding. "It's like bending waves," he says and the tin turns fluid, his
words having changed the property of metal for a moment, a break
from the work. Soon I'll move out here with Tina. He'll move into a
new rental, and I won't have his help I need.

"I like this, bending tin," I say to him, but he says, "Not me. I'd rather bend water, if that were possible."

All of this happens before we lose light, before we sweat dry and a rattler oxbows close, before the clouds let loose and the north wall is covered with old tin my friend Randy gave when he tore down the camp house on his farm. Tin, he and his father had painted so it wouldn't rust out and could still be of use.

OUT HERE

MAYBE THOREAU IS to blame for getting people started on this kind of living when he built his cabin on Walden Pond. Or maybe the dream goes deeper—that desire to make a shelter the way we want and to build it with our hands and sweat is what will truly sustain us. ◣

Hinge

TINA

Labor Day. Tent pitched under our roof
said camping. Brushing teeth and spitting
into the woods did too. But the refrigerator
smacked of luxury when I opened its door.
Luxury camping we said of our living
in the cabin as we built its walls.
Rain sometimes blew in through the studs
and tent mesh. Citronella sputtered away
at mosquitos as we cooked and ate supper.

Mornings we woke to butterflies banging
their slender bodies against panes
we had framed. They could not fathom light
could lie, mean anything but open path.
I offered my hand, carried each out,
feeling thin feet softly tap my palm,
watching wings hinge open and close,
until they lifted iridescence to sun.
A daily chore only those splendid
weeks of camping could afford.

Constellation JIM

The stars we wish for never make it to the ground—too many flood
lights encircle us, people afraid coyotes will turn into wolves into
burglars into devils. I want to tell them, seeing in your sleep won't
stop what's coming.

But maybe if we lived by an abandoned lake instead of in this tent on
a subfloor, we'd find stars there, the lake having soaked up night to
become a deep-mirrored glass.

To jump in would mean to startle the quiet dark open and speckle our
skin wet with million-year old light, would be to remake the sky with
us in it.

Showering at the Gym

TINA

It doesn't help arriving 15 minutes to close
when the lady at the desk sweeps up or walks
toward the door, keys in hand. Or to be sweaty,
wearing overalls, with sawdust filled cuffs,
and muddy boots. Or to say we're just showering,
not working out, we won't keep her past quitting
time. Or to tell her we don't have running water,
not yet, we're still building. Because the unhoused
shower in gyms, we tell ourselves we're not homeless
just showerless, wall-less, doorless, unplumbed.
Even when we arrive early, wear swimsuits, head
for the pool and hot tub to ease our aches,
that lady still smirks, "Coming for your shower?"
Though I trust water, lean back, spread arms, doze
a bit, believing I'll never drown, I still flinch
at her eye shadow, look her up and down, searching
for a waist, and cut my eyes at her scouring toilets.
When trying to keep our heads above water, we climb
whatever or whoever is in reach. Never helps swimming
for it, every man, woman, child for oneself.

September Prayer   JIM

Wake up, set hands to measure, saw-cuts and branch-scrapes scabbed
over, tendonitis in the right elbow getting tighter with each hammer
strike. This is the arm for power and chigger bites we never feel until
the red knots swell into itches at 3 a.m. For now, you square frames
in one corner. I lift glass into walls. We have to get dried-in by winter.
So hang with me, baby. Ride 'em Radiators to get warmed up when a
cold front shoots through. And look at the long rafters holding ceiling
boards steady. Don't you know impossible? Everything we've done so
far, this wood cut by steel, is coming into being.

Hatches

You were the one for hatches:
       hinging small doors
under the eaves
       as if to make cabinets
for stashing caches.

       I was for building walls,
for hanging doors. Strongholds
       against heat thieving winds.
But when you swung
       the hatches open,

the house sighed and I sighed
       with it. I knew then,
you are the one
       creating your own
likeness, a household
       that breathes sky in.

Stair Calculator

TINA

The front door steps had me hanging, leveling,
and fitting pre-cut stringers with treads.

But loft stairs needed calculating: dividing
the rise from floor to threshold by the sum

of the target-step height and the thickness
of the treads. Easy enough on the internet.

Impossible at the sawhorse, where boards varied
too much. Even my beloved $a^2 + b^2 = c^2$ failed

to reveal the angle to cut the stringers' ends.
So Jim rigged equations and checked our math

by the reality of boards. From the stair calculator
we used two bits of advice: a standard step is 7"

(except in New England where they step higher, unlike
Jim who won't ever stop shuffling across the floor)

and if, after recalculating, there must be a variation
in the rise between steps, place it at the end

or start of the stair. We chose the one at the bottom.
That, we figured, must be the beginning.

Turkey Vultures

TINA

All afternoon, vultures
     glide over the ridge,
turn and dive, tilting
     to rise and circle.

All day, no one holds the ladder
     as I climb up to keep
the skylight's pane in place,
     as you climb down for a drill,
more screws, something else we forgot
     or keep getting wrong.

Not one vulture flaps a wing.
     They just stretch out
wide into all that blows against them.

     Let that be you. Let that be me.
Let that wind fly right in our faces.

Visqueen

The cold keeps getting colder, we keep moving somehow. At least Vestal
is burning dogwood hot.

Tina's in town shopping for Christmas. We've stuffed glass into every
frame. Just not enough time to fill every opening.

So I get out the Visqueen and the stapler, start the work of sealing the
south wall clerestory.

Dried-in, I'll call it when done, even if that's not fully true.

Dried-in, will be my claim when wind hits Visqueen like striking a
boat's sail, waking us up at night from our dreams of bobbing on water.

But this home ain't going nowhere, I promise, and neither are we.

First Winter, the Cabin

TINA

doesn't know what it wants
to be. All night the Visqueen
       stapled to the clerestory breathes,
snaps, becomes a sail tacking us
       across a bristling sky.

Come morning, I poke cinders,
       stir Vestal into locomotive chug,
the cabin, a train bound
       for somewhere fast and warm,
smoke switchbacking
       all the way to glory.

The cabin doesn't know yet
       if it wants to stay, doesn't
know if it can trust the power
       poles reaching down, trying
hard to root us here.

STUTTER-STEP

LARRY BROWN HAD BEEN a fireman before becoming a writer. He wrote about people in Mississippi where he's from, and I was his student. One night, we were going over a story in class and everyone started tearing it apart.

Larry just listened and listened, then said, "It's good enough." Cut right through what everyone wanted that story to be.

I knew what he meant—perfection is for critics and disappointment. The real beauty is imperfection if you're open to it, if you're willing to look past your own prejudices and designs. ◣

Stutter-Step

We are all stop and start,
our home a tremble from hammer
and drill, the shriek of saw,
the waver of glass walls.
Never steady or still,

the walking sticks and praying
mantes judder across our porch
and deck. Like the root-bound
and breeze-rattled bluestem,
they quaver here to there.

When folks ask if we're done
with the cabin or the floors,
I answer we're somewhere
between halfway and never.
No doubt some wonder when

we'll be done going without
plumbing, living in one room.
Maybe they think I mean soon.
But I don't. And I don't prize
journey over destination.

We're here. We have arrived.
Each choice our own. We build
deck before bathroom,
still learning turn, sway,
how to fashion our own step.

Call it shillyshally
or lollygag. We step
to the rhythm of breeze
and breath of this place.

Weathermyth

My world now is a glass cabin I'm building with my wife on a ridge.
Lightning is plentiful. When it strikes close, our home shakes. If it
were to strike closer, our view of the woods would shatter.

Lightning struck a pine on Pop's farm in Spring '96, and a long branch
fell on four of his cows, one a favorite bull, black-and-white speckled.
Or maybe the blue gash he found burning in the trunk made the cows
gallop until their four hearts ruptured. Pop had seen them moseying
under thunder's crackle or cackle— "How you say it, depends on how
you hear it," he said. "I've never found truth in the exactness of things,
have you?"

Pop was close to a strike once in a pasture, said it felt as if he got
pushed by a wall. Sent him to the grass. Blackout. Damned headache.
He said, "Stings and strikes—that's where my memory takes hold."
I heard it different. He had a bald spot on the back of his head, and I
told my friends that's where lightning brought its haymaker. Just look
if you doubt. Haymakered him to the dirt. Then Pop got off the ground.

I remember walking behind him after I'd decided on my version of his
story—me, only so tall and staring at that spot way up. Meaning,
I had a lot of growing up to do. Meaning, he was more than just my
pop, a part of him had become myth. I was reading about the Greek
Gods, and Zeus kept throwing lightning bolts down at the county
farmers and their peanut fields, the boundary of my whole world then.

Pop, though a mortal, had been slammed in the head by Zeus, and he
walked as if that strike was nothing of a worry. The gods either get you
or they don't. You're either here or you're no longer.

Even though Tina refuses to look at our glass walls when trees start
bowing in a storm, she's not one to pray. And I am my father's son. But
when a storm turns into a polygon on the weather authority's map—
high winds, hail, a tornado starting its spin—we join the shared hush of
everyone in Alabama holding the same breath, sending the same prayer
to the sky—

> "Don't let my neighbor get lost in your fast winds coming.
> Don't let a body ride a road flash-flooded out. Please
> stop the wanderer from wandering under your sturdiest
> tree. And put us not on the path of a barrel-whistler, a
> trailer-tumbler. Just love us, deliver us, hold us tight."

Until there's damage to tell of, and we sigh, "Those poor people,"
about those taken, names not given so we can forget.

Rounds

After the storm, there are more power poles at Alabama Power for the taking. And my neighbor's building a house, this one for his son. The scraps they can't use, I can. So I get up. I make the rounds, checking for a call, looking for wood. These have become salvaging days, a kind of divining, like begging a story from old words.

I get to Alabama Power, cut one pole 15', length enough to bear the corner of a deck, what I've built over and over—the motions of it, the thoughts of it not yet real. The real is picking up this pole no one wants 'cause it's too gaffed from workers climbing to the transformer and lines. 'Cause the storm snapped it at its base. 'Cause it is ancient.

And yet, the pole will outlast me, preserved in harsher chemicals. I just have to get it in the truck, which takes a lot of summoning, hands on hips figuring, walking around delaying because dead weight is always more than I can reason. At some point, I have to lift.

Back home, I leave the pole in the truck. There's supper and sleep. By morning the carpenter bees are cutting rounds in the eaves. I sit on the stoop to write and sawdust sifts over these words. These very ones. Sawdust is a little bit heavier than pollen. And while I don't like carpenter bees chewing up the house wood, I understand their want for a home. The only end to want is bodies failing.

Built by Hand Ourselves

TINA

isn't to say we pulled ourselves up
by our bootstraps or these walls up
by scaffolding. Pop lent us that
and set us up with two lines of credit.
It means no crane, no backhoe,
not even a Bobcat, and no contractors,
just our muscle erected this glass cabin.

And ourselves really means Jim hefted
every board and beam here. Means Dylan
helped raise wall frames and rafters.
Means I shellacked boards, framed windows,
and built steps. Think of me as fry cook,
Jim as head chef, Dylan his sous.

Ourselves means Jim Owens bringing us power
poles to hold up our floor. Means Madi digging
post-holes and building our poop bin. Means
Jeff and Nancy wrangling rafters into the sky.
Means Tom, my neighbor in Oregon, telling us
how to insulate an exposed beam ceiling.

Ourselves is Dave McCrae wiring the power
from the meter to the breaker box, shoving
our woodstove up ramp and over threshold.
And Traci giving us our first rain barrel
and cat. Aunt Trish and Uncle Gene giving us
windows, Ted and John, boards. Nick splitting
red cedar for our deck rails, offering up
every windfall for firewood. Ourselves is that

single breeze on the stickiest day when chiggers
swelled our every crease and we could have
boiled right over if it hadn't blown
across our necks just then. Ourselves isn't
Whitman's multitudes, isn't the shoulders of giants
Einstein acknowledged he stood on. Ourselves are
that many, that huge, but they are all around us
still, real, and forever lending us a hand.

Shelf Weather

I forget people's names, what they tell me about themselves so brightly. But the bear in me has a long reach when it comes to weather. It knows, like all ferociousness, this wind can only cut at the sun for so long. With my face hurting from two weeks of sick, and my mind stashing words far away, my hands take over. They push the thick shaving of a poplar through the table saw. Slice it thinner, sand it finer. They cut legs from crepe myrtle, sand down the knobs of black mold and bark, then swing the legs out like dancing to catch the right balance. That poplar fell on the powerline two winters ago. It made everyone's household go quiet for a day. My neighbor, Nick, pruned the crepe myrtles last July and gave a bundle to me, he said, "to make use of." Now the wind pins the sun low. The bear shrugs into wander, looking for a thick-leaved trough of hibernation. And I am without a helping hand. I lean a side of the new shelf against an old shelf of shoes I made in summer. I steady the loose pieces of wood in place. One more twist to square the corners. Then the new legs step out, ready to run.

Pliers

— for P.Y. —

I no longer want a miniature made with a thin orange carpet, a
green vinyl couch, and a tiny pair of pliers atop a tv whose knobs are
broken off. I no longer need a footlocker set by the door as if packed
with Dad's workweek denim, or a bay window overlooking the other
trailers in the park, and piers reaching out into the slough like bridges
gone nowhere. Not because the Thorne Miniatures are said to be
two parts fantasy to one part history and there's no fantasy in my
childhood living room. It's because of the pliers, the ones you said you
needed to turn the broken knobs of your tv like we did. Pliers you and
your brothers squabbled over like they were a remote control made
of diamonds. Pliers my dad used to pull my first tooth because he
couldn't get "aholt" of it otherwise. Pliers Dad once took to work with
him leaving us watching PBS until he returned that weekend. You
didn't say if you used pliers in an apartment or a shotgun house in
India or Canada or on the farm you mentioned in Pennsylvania. No
matter, your pliers made my history feel universal, I now want them
made gigantic, able to reverse the scale of Thorne Miniatures and other
rooms of affluence. Made into a monument to how hordes of us make
do, take hold, fight even, to change one station to another.

Without Varnish

TINA

I feign interest in shellac—
              the poly or linseed oil—
       that hardware men swear
will keep a cedar's heart true
              to the red-purple revealed
       by a saw's quick teeth.

Like trying another angle
              or a different lens to take
       a sunset's picture, nothing
really captures that color
              or keeps it from fading.
       I know. I've tried.
To avoid seeming rude,
              I don't tell them

       it's better held like the toads
Jim sometimes brings me.
              His hands are a small home
       that he opens into mine.
I feel the toad's silk throat
              billow against my palm.
       When I part fingers to let her go,
I catch the copper of her eyes.

Tongue and Groove JIM

The heart pine boards come from H's house. Me and my children
crowbarred and hammered them loose from his ceiling ten Decembers
ago. We couldn't see then the universe under the layer of fireplace
smoke and field dust the wind had brought inside for a hundred years
and settled down—I'm sanding that smoke and dust out of the wood
now, freeing up the logjam of tree rings so the red and purplebrown
hardened sap might open downstream into estuary of floor.

Spontaneous Combustion

TINA

Now that smoke braids up from the bucket
of oily rags, I want to let them smolder
into flicker, blaze into downright burn.

Not because you snickered, "Old wives' tale"
and asked if we really can trust the science
taught at my grade school. Sure, this smoke

vindicates my nagging and the oil can's warning
that after we oiled our floor planks our rags
would steep warmer than the sun's glare.

Though I said, chin lifted, "I am an old wife,
I'm yours," I didn't believe it could be so simple,
that laying down one rag on another would work

such magic in a bucket half full of water.
Hold on now, it won't burn down all we built
to learn how hot and how high this can go.

List of Things

JIM & TINA

Chainsaw needs to go to the shop today. Need to get water from Blue Spring today. Need to sit in a warm-hot tub of water wearing Levi's so they'll shrink. I'm losing heat and daylight. Should've done this over summer. Need to do the dishes before Tina goes to the store. Need to fix the southeast corner of the cabin where the wood has started to rot from the oak branch. Too much rain this year. Need to sit outside in the cowboy bathtub and watch bees. They're zooming, getting ready for winter.

TODAY'S TO DO

____ Feed the mother

____ Walk dog

____ Deadhead zinnias and marigolds to keep them going, blooming, feeding bees till frost says gone

____ Cut okra and tomatoes, roast them for supper

____ Sweep once Jim loads up the water bottles, takes them to be refilled, get at that bit of floor for once

____ Mix hummingbirds some sugared water

____ Mail bills, postcards, Netflix

____ Drop cans at Cross Recycle and paper at the library bin

____ Get groceries

____ Tend tadpoles

____ Scoop out bees in rain buckets and tadpole water

____ Forget dusting, windows, laundry

____ Hang hammock, write and read, breathe

Least I'm Not as Picky as a Carolina Wren

TINA

Though Jim must build us another sink,
a third one, with a shallow charm
to ease our aching backs. I insist
he lower the bar to counter-height
for chopping and rolling out dough
without cricking my neck. And I often
say copper gutters would look best.

But I'm not after a whole other house
like this wren making her mate build
nest after nest until one suits her.
All the others, whose leaves he wove
lacy and soft, and all that labor, is left
to be blown away. I'd rather Jim build
me the river I crave. But this is all

we got in us, we say, shaking our heads
at how we shouldn't have depended on
silicone, that filler of fake tits,
to seal our walls. Making do requires
bracing the foundation posts, sistering
rafters, adding fascia boards to block
rain outwitting walls. So I am demanding

no more experiments, no more makeshift,
the rest has to be made for keeps.
I think through closets and pantry,
figure just how I want the sink, I swear
to make do if it's not just right.

This isn't settling. This isn't
an anything-is-enough-if-you-know-how
-poor-you-are sort of thing. Look
at how even the pickiest wren
chooses the nest built in our eaves.

Always and Absolutely

JIM

Philip Johnson's glass house in Connecticut says, "Look at me." We do and find Johnson was once a nazi sympathizer. After he became an architect, others vouched that he had atoned. So look at the design now, how the glass, that liquid river, shoots the light straight through as if to make him clean.

Pop's house is called the glass house of Wilcox County. One half is cinder block facing his driveway and one half is floor to ceiling windows overlooking swamp. A girl I dated said the house was unfinished. No, he built it simple on purpose. The cinder block keeps you from looking in. Once inside, the plate glass keeps you looking out. Pop has never wanted to draw attention, never wanted "to embarrass his kids" he tells me often. Without the cinder block, a neighbor could stay outside long enough to watch Pop be who he is, which is gay, which could lead to breaking in and burning down. Johnson, who was also gay, came from money, which allowed him to purchase an insulation Pop's never had. Pop chose the rural community he comes from, always and absolutely. He tells me too many times to count, "You are better than no one and no one is better than you."

And us? The woods hide our glass cabin in Alabama, a nest in a low branch you could drive by everyday, invisible. Neighbors warn, it's not a question of if you'll be robbed but when as if we store our worth like our bees. To steal it, you have to drive into country unfamiliar. Have to walk through pines and broadleaf oaks, past cedars and wild plums. Once you've broken in, you have to make the walk out. At some point, a branch will snag and turn you until you see yourself in windows framed by hand. Know that we didn't set out to design a house of glass, and we know the story of stones. We built what is ours from what others handed down for free.

Drill or Haul

Heavy trucks rut our road,
hauling a drill, pipe wider
than me, and tank after tank
of water for cooling bits.
All week that drill drones
on like an unreachable itch
until I wonder if the neighbors-
to-be dowsed, if they'll hit water
soon or need to try again,
and if the trees they pushed over
and into a pile will burn off
tonight, clearing the air
of smoke if not racket.

You set your lean limbs
and fox face to refilling
Ruby's tire and transmission,
lift the IBC tote to her
truck bed, drive down
to the water authority, haul
water up, carry it in jugs
for our showers, dishes,
and hands. You equal all
the units of work it takes
for others to have water
pour at the turn of a knob.
And you work without noise
or killing trees or probing
dirt for hundreds of feet.

Your work is more exquisite,
worth more. It's why
joule is said like jewel.
And Jim like gem.

Neighbor on the Dirt Road

JIM

—for Ginny—

She says things don't look good. Says, "I got things set right with the Lord. Nothing to worry about there." Says she and her man are going on a cruise for adults. "You know how children are. They like to run all over the place and get sick." She laughs.

"I ain't doing chemo again," she says. "Not worth it. Doctor says it might give me a few months. Might." She says she's got six. She says she's not ready to leave her man, and that's when she starts to cry.

Last month she was feeling good. She said the chemo was done. Said she was retiring from her job in a year. She laughed, "I am oh so ready." She said, "There are things I want to do."

May

You will not get this day again, blackberry winter, the hawk flying over. In February, the junipers were spring born. Now, cedar-apple rust galls have turned orange. I thought the galls, hanging from the ends of branches, were the seeds of cedars. I thought the hawk in February would come down eventually. Surely the wind had to stop holding up its wings. But lost in my measuring is how much the sky can hold.

Things Just Wear Out

A TEXT POP SENT

My heart valves won't close properly, and I'm too old for
surgery. The backflow of blood can't get oxygen, explained
the cardiologist. Fluid buildup causes swelling that
thwarts blood's reach. It causes my stomach to bloat and
gives me shortness of breath. A chain reaction. Since
you can't repair 'em, you throw pills at 'em to offset the
malfunction. When I looked at the echo image, that
backflow of blood didn't make me feel any secure. I'm
surprised these tiny pills are doing the trick so far.

THE REPLY I CAN'T SEND

Remember when Hurricane Michael cut through the
farm? I drove south until I could saw trees off your roof
and out of your driveway. Sometimes it seems, I built a
house in Alabama so I would know how to take care of
yours. Our homes require constant care. I would fix those
valves in you myself, but I'm better at working wood than
heart. I'm afraid I'll make a mess keeping you alive. I
don't want to see limits—possibility is where I'm most
secure—yet I think of you dying. Happens on evenings
when I'm tired. I don't know what happens after I can't
talk to you anymore. The day of your passing, the world
will stop spinning long enough for me to fall to the
ground but not into it. And that's as far as I've come.

The Flowering Pear

TINA

never fruits. Yet each March blossoms burst
along every branch raised over our neighbors'
bed of daffodils and glinting windmill art.

Its pale petals screen dark limbs, a bridal veil
drawing attention to what's obscured.
Alive and flowering, it's unlike the windthrows

or widow-makers Nick usually offers us to cut
and haul to our woodpile. Generous to a fault,
he grins as if we're doing him the favor.

He says it has been pretty and still is. Tells us
they planted it on their wedding day. But now
that Judy says it's invasive, it has to go.

Married five years to their twenty, what do we know
of when to hew and root out a beginning,
of how to tend what has been cultivated since?

We know oak burns steady. Dogwood catches quick.
Sweetgum is nearly impossible to split. Poplar
puts out too little heat. And flowering pear?

What else can we say? But that we need fire
and wood to feed it. We'll haul it home,
fill our stove, learn something of how it burns.

February Prayer

We pass the time with firewood hauling, afterward with beer as we walk the dog. The days, even the uneasy ones because of the cold, we slip through by writing and working to stay warm, to ready ourselves for spring. And they are gone fast, this day into that one. There is no difference. Except the sun staying out longer when the rains let up, except the lizards appearing in a hibernation stupor. We place them on trees to spare them the dog and the cat. Then back to the next words, the next carrying, splitting, sawing, walking, crude drawings of what to build next. The days are a list of what to do, of the cabin shifting into home. Always there are pauses—only in retrospect does time glide. Each sheet of glass frames another pause, a gathering up of the whole curved stretch of sun and the single place it holds in that moment, where the moon was last night, where we can never point to exactly, again.

Mud Baby

TINA

I am no poet, but just mud
—GEORGE E. OHR

Our house is a tall man.
It is the serrano pepper
baked atop the buttermilk
cornbread. It is the poof
of lichen a lacewing larva
sports as bouffant. It is
a cloud so shot through
with light the sunbeams
fan out like a peacock tail.

It is the song "At Last" sung
now and forever by Etta James.
It is a desire path deer cut
through briers. It is that
cucumber scent that could be
kudzu bloom or copperhead
or an unexpected volunteer.
Our house is quartz outcrop.

It is a denim quilt pieced
from cut-offs and work-shirts.
It is that glorious week of spring
that teases us each February.
Our house is a George Ohr pot,
one we would know is a mistake
to sell, so we'd chase the buyers
down, throw their money

in their faces, shouting,
"We've changed our minds,
now give us our mud baby back!"

Our house is a mud baby
despite all the glass
and wood. It is tended
like a newborn, handheld
as its built. It is mud
always sticking to our step.

WATERWORKS

250 GALLONS

WE PURCHASE drinking water from Blue Spring up in Blountsville twenty gallons at a time. Each five gallon jug holds over forty pounds of water. Each jug, made of glass, weighs another ten. We haul water for cleaning purposes from the local water authority, 250 gallons at a time in an IBC tote on the back of Ruby, our '98 Dodge truck. Our cube-shaped tote gives us a sense of the size and shape of water. When we read statistics about how much a person flushes per day or week or month, we imagine cubes set side by side or stacked high like a beanstalk.

We wish we had a spring. A well won't do—too expensive when wells around here can run dry during droughts and summer, anytime the water-table drops. It made us curious about Sally Branch. We hoped she might lead us to a spring on our property.

Ruby manages to chug uphill to home, though I'm not sure for how much longer. Then the over-a-ton water gets gravity fed through garden hoses to a second tote that sits on stilts at the southeast corner of the cabin. Takes about four hours for the transfer.

From it, I fill blue plastic jugs, carry them inside, and pour them into a ceramic croc that has a spigot for washing

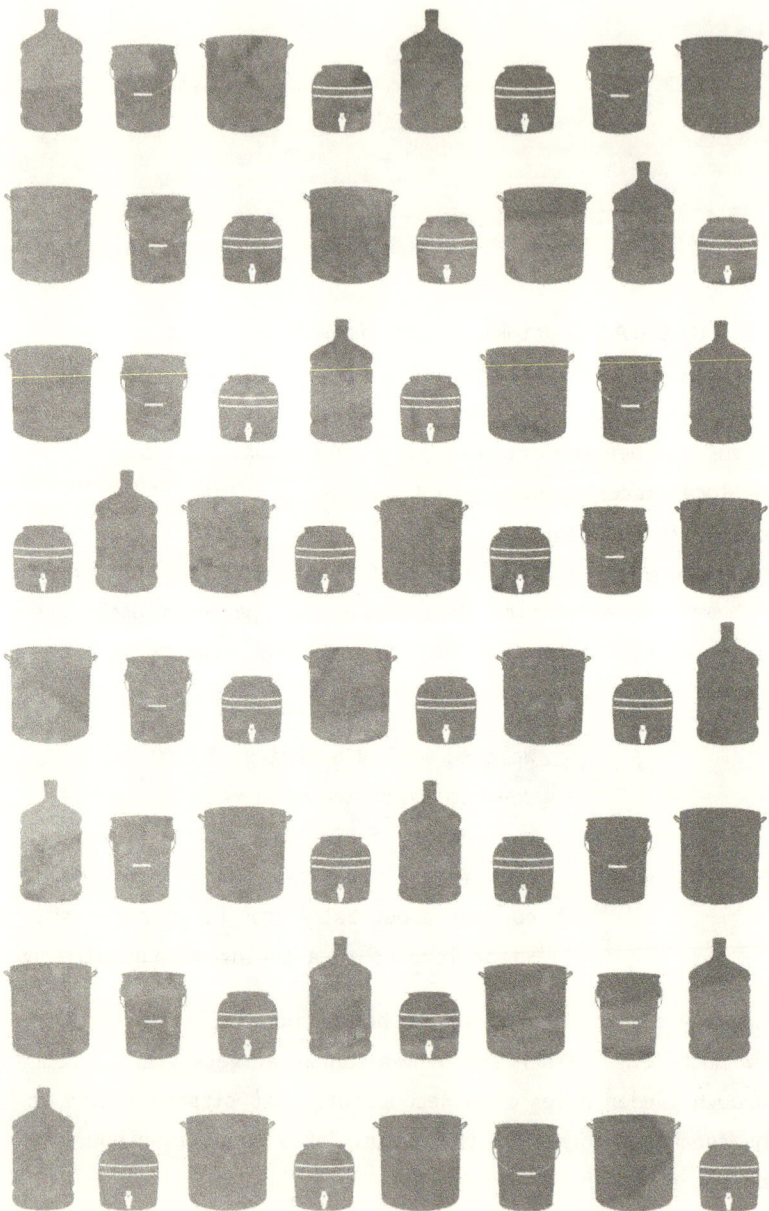

250 GALLONS

hands. The bucket underneath the sink has to be emptied
several times a day.

> Sally is the closest body of water to
> us, but to say "body" feels like an
> exaggeration for a creek prone to dry up
> if there's no run-off from Cherty Ridge
> on one side and our Hydrangea on the
> other. If Sally were human, some would
> say she disappeared whenever she turned
> sideways. In reality she switches not
> just left and right but in and out of the
> ground.

I heat water in a stockpot on the stovetop and pour it into
two stainless steel basins to wash dishes. Heated-up water
is also poured into an old cowboy bathtub Pop gave us so we
can soap up and get clean. Because even a half-full tub is
too heavy to carry outside, I have to scoop the after-bath
liquid out. Or I fill a stockpot on the deck, drop a heating
coil down inside, so we can use a camping shower to wash in
the noon sun, at sunset, under the Little Dipper.

> I imagine Sally as a slip of a girl, the
> skin and bones sort, a heroin-thinned
> model, who would call her thrift-store
> duds vintage.

For our washing machine, I collect rain off the roof in
buckets and using an old cloth, filter it—full of pollen,
straw, bugs, and leaves—into the washing machine for our
clothes. Takes twenty gallons for one load. Then Tina pins
the clothes to the line to dry. On stormy days, she brings
them in and hangs them from the sleeping loft.

We talk about gutters and a cistern—that's the dream. But until then, I drive Ruby to the authority. I go to Blue Spring. For the clothes, we give encouragement to clouds. So I know the time it takes to haul and carry water. And I know the weight of it, how much is needed to wash hands and clothes and clean a body of the dirt and sawdust and sweat of each day.

> And Sally is decked out. Wildflowers blossom along her banks, while plastic and silk flowers hang from limbs and exposed roots. Foam cones still holding wire "stems" gather in dry bends. That's oddly pretty unlike the submerged dart board, vented backs of TV sets, the video tape that's unwound along the trees like a black police line, the toilet seat half buried where the creek bed has gone dry, the deflated basketball, the rug hanging over a log. So much trash in Sally Branch, I can't gather it all, much less haul it up the steep ridge home.

When I'm in B town and turn the faucet on in a store restroom or someone's house, water shoots out so fast, I jump. I try to wash my hands quick to stop it from disappearing. And I wonder about the ones who don't have running water like me. I bet when they turn on a faucet, they jump, too. I bet they turn breathless, anxious because of the rushing and the waste. Tina likes to say, "Inconvenience pushes us to conserve." Convenience leads to neglect.

> Sally, like all water, reveals us, reflects our image. Even what goes to the dump, water carries back out. Water outwits us

and whatever wall we put up. It erodes
the line we draw between ourselves and
those callous enough to dump and litter.

Until we chose to live this way, I didn't think about the
weight of water or see my hands as the hands of those who
can't get water easily. They're struggling to get enough food,
too, struggling to find heat and shelter.

Now I see myself in what I ignore, let
blow away because I'm too tired to chase
it down. I am the grocery sack I accept
because the bag boy gives me grief when
I say I don't want one. I'm the gum-
ball machine toys I buy because they're
cheap, fun for a day. And I'm those hotel
samples that I adore. I'm even the funeral
flowers and video tape strung down a
creek far from where anyone lives.

And that weight stays with me in my half-dreaming. Wherever
it lifts into a lightness is where Tina is. The cabin we are
building wraps our love around our necessity—another way
that we are lucky.

And Sally Branch, that thrift-store hottie,
she keeps telling us this stuff ain't holy,
ain't nothing but what you give me. Watch
me wear it, flaunt it. It is the fashion.
Don't you know who I'm wearing? It's you.
Even out here, it's all about you. ◣

Solar Power

"But you're off-grid,"
some say-ask when learning
we live without running water.

I should tell them we're not
set up for solar. Our roof
slopes west to northwest
like the ridge, not south
as it should. Each spring
our hickory reaches farther
over the roof, and our oak
shades more west windows.

Even the Solar Guy said
if we topped all our trees
we wouldn't get enough light.
We can't afford the $50K
set up costs. We don't want
to pay the $5 per Kilowatt
Alabama Power charges
for use of the sun.
Tree rich, cash poor,
we're not set on
our trees dying.

"No, we have power,"
is easier to say,
though it leaves me
watching their faces

fall. I'm sure
how they see us seeps
down because water,
even saving it,
always sinks
to the lowest level.

Alaska

The buckets underneath the roof fill with rainwater I will pour into
the washing machine tomorrow to clean Tina a week's worth of
clothes. She refuses me an electric dryer. She says, "Not as long as the
sun is free." So laundry is for clear days and windy days, for pinning
on the line.

But tonight the hickory pinches the moon between its branches, and
moonlight is spilling into air so humid it forms raindrops taken to
pearling along the metal edge of the roof. When the pearls get heavy,
they fall into the buckets causing water-light to zig and zag like a
water strider, like a current of sky I saw once.

That night the Northern Lights fell too far for anyone to gather. I
wanted to follow them across the continent to Alaska. I was sturdy
enough to go, but when I stepped outside, everyone on the library steps
was trapped in awe and I stood still.

In our glass cabin, currents of solitude work different. The moon
turns the loft's ladder blue by quarter so we can see to step to the floor.
Turkey vultures and hawks map thermals above Sally Branch. The
sun falls early in December here. In July, late here over Cherty Ridge.
When lightning burns a strike into a pine, I check my body for smoke
and fire. And though I am less sturdy I still want that pull telling me,
"Walk to Alaska," so I can rest close to the Northern Lights unwinding
the earth above its glaciers.

Down from the Cabin

TINA

Sally Branch rushes brown and high
with last night's storm. Glass shards
blue along her bank and sandstone
gleams with runoff's spit shine. Today
the red tips of maples barely whisper
bud, blossom, new leaf. And that flitting
swallowtail isn't a kite or a flower taken
by flight. It isn't the shape of my fancy.
The swallowtail cannot make today tomorrow.
It is only right now dusting the yellow jasmine.
Right now Sally Branch is a road and I am
a mustang convertible, red, the fastest.
Now the water is a galloping horse I'm offering
an apple. Tree trunks cast bars of shadows
across fallen leaves but hold nothing back.
When Sally Branch becomes the Milky Way
tonight, and me a firefly, I'll say, "my glint
calls out to yours," the way the water
in me reaches for these rapids.

Fourteen Rivers

THE FOURTEENTH RIVER

pours through when we open the hatches in October and curls cold
'round our warm bones so we might sleep into balance.

Come morning it makes arches of light on the new floor. Brighter and
brighter, the sun leafs with shadow, and all I want is to cut shape out
of this light.

THE THIRTEENTH RIVER

was made in May out of big leaf hickory and silver maple. When we go walking, their dying leaves spin like paper fires into our hands.

THE TWELFTH RIVER

comes from what Tina said—"Land is a current contoured and
bending." I find rivulets in the bark of trees, along the backs of toads.
My own skin carries the silt of river beds.

THE ELEVENTH, TENTH, AND NINTH RIVERS

are where I lived when I needed to be drawn downstream.

Grain barges and coal barges dotted the Ohio. I made a perch of lost hours watching them disappear.

I took my children to the Deerfield to make their feet into fins before their toes grew cramped with cold.

And when I crossed the Mississipp, a bald eagle swung in front of my windshield, a small fish in its talons. The eagle's wings beat, the fish thrashed silver to get loose. Everything before me living was dying, then lifted away.

THE EIGHTH RIVER

is the one through the heart. It says, I am the only machine that
matters because I refuse to stop.

THE SEVENTH RIVER

is the Coosa that Tina grew up on, swam in, made a barge out of a
dented freezer door to float on, so she could read books and keep away
from shore.

Her part of the Coosa was a dammed lake for Alabama Power, for a
fisherman's paradise. Her father loved to fish it before his stroke.
That's how Tina first knew a river—fast currents brought to a slow
summer waltz.

THE SIXTH RIVER

is the one I will cross or be carried in. I do not know which going is better, but my legs didn't make me a long-jumper. Boats make me seasick and I am not a good swimmer like Tina, but I can manage either for a while.

THE FIFTH RIVER

diving hawks slice in half so sure, so fast my hands can never catch.

THE FOURTH RIVER

is the way people walked Saturday at the fall fair, everyone in a
current, then all at once, blackbirds turning without knowing where
to go next.

THE THIRD RIVER

is the Alapaha at the edge of Pop's farm where he and his friends rode
bikes to muddy themselves with laughter. I have walked there to see
Pop down in the current so I might find who he was then, so he might
swim young.

THE SECOND RIVER

thunderstorms from the clouds all summer.

THE FIRST RIVER

is our branch, Sally. She gets loud in evenings after a good rainmaker.
Tells us to pull up chairs and listen.

Coosa

              I did fall
for the slow summer waltz
              of a dammed river,
wind ruffling her skin
              more than her own current,
fell for how I floated
              all damn day, dozed even,
without drifting beyond
              sight of my pier.
Coosa more coo than rush.
              I don't tell Jim
that all night, my body fell,
              eddying into swirl.
Dams needn't break for her
              to sweep me into sway.

And I don't tell him
              he's wrong about me
reading library books
              while floating the Coosa
on a dented walk-in
              cooler door. The rage
that summer for being
              buoyant as a barge
and just $8 from a guy
              working the factory.
But I did climb into the pine
              closest to the shore
and read in branches where
              willow flies swarmed.

And I read on the pier
   Dad built of metal poles
and railroad ties to last
   forever. Close enough
to where I launched
   the door, splashing
its gleam to keep it
   from scorching palms
and bare thighs.
   I couldn't risk paying
for wet books new or lent.

   I don't tell Jim that
I want him like I want you
   to see me aboard a door
charting Huck Finn
   escapades, glistening
in the same borrowed
   words y'all read. Look.
See it's the same
   shimmer, river ripples,
a trailer's pleated walls.

Visiting Walden Pond

Where trees marigold the shore,
       swimmers clad in wetsuits
tow bladders of breath across
       the pond and back, so regular
it appears they follow lanes painted
       along the bottom, so serious
it seems we must join their current
       or keep out. We still wade in,
our bare arms and legs goose-pimpling.
       Jim wades out then dunks himself
with a baptism whoop. I give up waiting
       for fish to come kiss my ankles
when a woman says, "Look, a crawfish.
       At least one's left." Frog-kicking out
of the swimmers' right-of-way, I float,
       face the sky and its clouds,
knowing water has my back.
       I imagine Henry living here
all the seasons twice over. Not long,
       I've heard some say, as if
not enough for all he claims.
       I doubt a decade in our cabin
is enough for them either. It isn't
       for us. But it's plenty
to find our way here, dousing
       ourselves, one way
or another, in this deep water.

Ephemeral Pool

TINA

means it won't always be
here. Means puddle said
in a highfalutin way. Means
the sun and soil will Shop-Vac
this water like these dirt daubers
and bees, like the coyote
and turkey who tracked
through the middle
to drink it up.

Biodiverse is another way
of saying rain pooled
on a dirt road atop a ridge
in Alabama. It's a nod
of respect to tadpoles
shimmying and turning
their opal bellies up
to catch the light
and the mosquito larvae
flicking tail against head
to dive and surface.

Ephemeral means that
in a single drop
there's a galaxy
of single-celled creatures
thriving inside
delicate silica walls
just as they did
when dinosaurs splashed
through puddles.

Their bodies are glass houses
is what some say.
Maybe we should all say,
when we look to diatoms
and ask how to love our neighbors
enough to keep
from throwing any stones.

GOING FERAL

I GREW UP using a septic system and hated it. There were
times when the underground tank got full. The water and
the black smelly, sandy crud backed up into the bathtub in
the old house, and I was the one told to clean it out. So
I didn't want a septic tank at Hydrangea. Besides, it takes
more than a gallon for a single flush, and we don't have
running water.

Instead, we use a bucket system where poop and pee and
vegetable scraps go into a paint bucket and get covered with
carbon—peat works best for us—to take up the odor. I built a
wooden box with a toilet seat and lid to house the bucket-in-
use. Think of it as a cat litterbox for people. Once we fill
up ten to twelve buckets, I empty them into one of our above-
ground 5' x 5' poop bins. After a filled bin "rests" for a year,
I wheelbarrow its contents to the garden for fertilizer.

Fancy composters that look like regular toilets cost at least
a thousand. Hard to imagine ever having so much money we can
splurge on a fancy toilet. A bucket, now that we can afford.

Most people don't want to spend so much time with their own
crap, but I like how this simple system works as advertised.
The main thing is the maintenance. And it requires someone
strong enough to lift heavy buckets. Tina worries about this,
especially when we get older, and reminds me, "You don't have
to fill them all the way up." ◣

The Thing About
Composting Toilets

TINA

I love volunteers, sprouting thick
	as grass from our compost, a variety
of tomato we ate and didn't sow.
	I marvel that they came from us,
through us, like children growing
	stronger for it. They overtake
every start we plant, bear fruit
	like grandkids feeding us more wonder
at all we didn't notice before.
	Wonder at how much more animal—
way more than sex—this soil is
	at coupling us with earth.

An Accounting of Birds

TINA

New study finds birds give people as much
happiness as money
—ANAGHA SRIKANTH, *The Hill*

It takes money to make money,
      and birds to weave grass
and hair into nests or daub mud pockets
      onto cliffsides. It takes
a summer tanager turning red
      to woo a delicate yellow mate
and a nestling blue jay jumping
      to evade the snake. He squawks,
as I settle him in a cedar
      for his parents to bring home.
It takes fledglings retreating
      to their nest moments before
the storm swoops in.
      And vultures turning gorgeous
circles no matter how gray
      the sky gets, how hideous
their scrawny necks.
      Any bird in the bush
is worth more than all
      the tender we might hold.

Easement

— for Tina —

The easement for the powerline, I turned into a meadow. "As if you
had a thing to do with what's growing there," you say while we walk.
So I talk about the clover and rye I seeded. I point to where I cut down
small pines to make an airstrip for the bees. Two hives survived the
spring-swarming.

Then we hear a cry in the bluestem and climb from the clay road the
rains have washed and rutted. We go looking, the dog the first to stop.
Just beyond her nose is a baby rabbit curled up in a snake. Hard to tell
design and color so deep in the stems and no rattle, no flat, poisonous
head, but I'm not sure.

"What can we do?" you say. "What do we have a right to do?" I say and
feel life slipping from what you want. I run home, get a shovel, return
and raise it, guessing where to strike. Miss. The snake slips out fast
and the baby rabbit, paralyzed from the squeeze, draws in the quiet
of dying.

It does no good to help things, though you have spent summer cradling
fledglings that fell too early out of their nests, dartings that hit the
church glass on the west wall. You lay them in boxes, in dish towels
made of colors that matched their wings, and set them on the deck
until they repaired, or a parent arrived to nudge them out, or I took
them to bury inside a ring of cedar and pine.

That ring is where I go now to raise the shovel. Our cherty ground
never wants to open but eventually I dig up a root-full wedge. I lower
the rabbit, cover it, place rocks over loose dirt to keep coyotes from the

new dead. And I say words for the branches to take to the heartwood where time on this ridge is preserved in rosin, purple and slow. Care is what we have to offer here and what we count on.

Victory Lap

"I made a meadow," Jim says
        of the easement that Alabama Power
cleared decades ago. Nevermind
        the fleabane daisies and the lady
slippers, the black-eyed Susans
        and sweet peas, the bluestem
and the rest that took root before
        he trimmed briers, pulled up
poison ivy, planted clover.
        "I made a meadow," he says again.

I tell him I teach tadpoles and toadlets
        to breathe, to beach themselves
along the waterline of my casserole dish
        for the food I sprinkle there.
I teach them to try out air, to emerge
        from water, their first world. Me.

Long ago, God talked Water into making heaven
        of her belly, lighting it up
with stars. And then he told her, "Oh Water,
        pull yourself together, let land
appear." He kept after her, saying,
        "Water, sweetheart, fill yourself
with fish, the air with birds.
        See how it is good? How good
it makes me? How good it is to say so?"

Indicator Species

Frogs and toads mean good
habitat. Bears would mean even better.
        When the neighbors suggest
I take pepper spray to the Smoky Mountains,
        I get they don't want bears
denning in our woods like I do.
        So I raise tadpoles as if
I could rig indications
        the way my aunt rigged
sewing machines to sew scrubs faster.
        She was paid by the piece.
I scoop tadpoles out of a drying puddle
        and huddle them into casserole dishes
filled with water and sand enough
        for a beach as if I am good,
as if I alone can make us
        good. As if my neighbors
won't mind the mosquito larvae
        wriggling out their wings.
As if I am that human, able
        to take the world as is.
You know, claws and all.

The End of Plastic Netting JIM

I smell something dead but can't see it. Think it's a bird caught in the
plastic netting we stretched over the garden, a cheap cover to keep
them out. They get in anyway. Once, we found the head of an Indigo
Bunting.

So I look for a glint of blue. I look for flies. But it's not until I get to
weeding and thinning sunflowers, squash on the backrow that I hear
the ushers buzz. Above me, a black racer had climbed up to thread a
loop. But its body, bloated with a field mouse, couldn't.

And it is karma, the bad kind. Last week I found a speckled king
inching through a piece of plastic netting I'd thrown on the ground.
Each inch gained, the net dug in tighter. So I called Tina and she
worked a scissor point under the mesh lines while I held the body still.
Then off the snake went into the woods more irritated than thankful.

I cut the racer down. Rip and pull the netting, bundle it, haul it to
the trash. I'm done with the rest of the day. But shame has little use
when you're aware of what you need to do and don't. We're not made of
plastic, and we sure as hell won't live forever.

Cliché

JIM

A friend visiting us from up north said she was told you can no longer write about trees—too much has been written about them. But, she said, every time she hikes uphill into a horseshoe of birches she becomes breathless, her vocal box folding-unfolding the mechanisms of winter, and "How can I not write of something so inexhaustibly a part of me?"

In summer is when I miss the birches up north, finding them white like long legs of snow showing off knee-dirt and black-gnarls where I once lived. I tied a rope-swing to a birch bent out into a field so I could swing my children. That birch dipped and set like Frost said.

Maybe because we carry cold for only a few months here, our birches tend to resemble our rivers made of mud and straw and peach light and bluing gnarls. Think of each trunk as a freshet after a storm, how water rolls, strikes roots, takes rocks and dirt downstream. Think the first note of any word striking your tongue against the back of your teeth, just like birches forked at the wind.

Shadows Now

       The lamp on my desk attracts
the praying mantis who turns
       in the wavering way
of twigs, between katydid, moth,
       and walking stick.
Like Henri, I see the mantis
       as god horse or maybe goddess
for how she twists her neck,
       takes me in, then steps
behind the lampshade.
       She's saying blessings
in the shadows now,
       not for her supper,
but the length of her gait,
       not for light,
and never for me.

Lay at My Feet

TINA

a chorus line of quail
to wind around the saplings that edge
        our powerline easement,
a plagueful of toads, so every footfall
        sends five hopping away,
springing my toes free to roam this ridge.

        Bring me firewood aglow
with foxfire before it lights my stove.
        Bring me owls hooting from love
and a Bob White to fill the gloaming
        with his name. I will whistle it back
just as he called it, responding
        to each call with courtesy.
Bring me enough sumac to carry bees
        through summer's dearth and crows
through winter. Bring me widening patches
        of wild iris and fire pink.

Let Ozark chinquapins unfurl leaf.
        Let them burst burs.
Let them hail chestnuts down,
        washing our ridge
with an abundance unseen in a century.
        Bring me the same
resistance, fostered by hand
        in seedling after seedling,
so I can overcome my own blights.

And when I'm in the dark, bring me
the light that isn't mine, pitch-black
        pulsing with lightning bugs,
the Milky Way glittering through
        our skylight. Let me see us
mirrored in this and every puddle.

A Pair of Hawks

JIM

West of the cabin, they keep circling, spinning wind the crows don't like while two pins on the clothesline hold up the shoulders of your favorite blouse. An hour ago, I unbuttoned the top pearl button and lifted, and in the lifting, static deviled your hair. Now the washed pearls are out drying, and a pine's needles are showing through a gap of chestnut-oak branches. Every one of its sawtooth leaves snapped off in yesterday's storm. But the dogwoods' purple-red holds still. And above, cloud joins cloud to notch the blue field over the ridge. That's where red-tails are leading crows to sun until I have nothing left of this day to catch.

THE APOCALYPSE

You can plant yourself forever
and still wobble every storm.
— RICHARD HUGO

I COME BY THE apocalypse honest, or it was nurtured by the Seventh-day Adventist Church I grew up in. Its doctrine teaches the world is coming to an end with famine and floods and earthquakes and disease and war. Not only that, the true believers will be persecuted and will need to run for the hills during "the end times" that will precede the return of Christ. I found all this fascinating, which may mean, I directed my utter horror into an obsessive fascination with how people might handle apocalypses, a fascination that compels me to devour apocalyptical movies and tv shows and novels, such as the ones written by my husband, Jim, who tolerates my apocalypticalness because it, in at least small ways, attracted me to him. ◣

May the Apocalypse Come in Early Spring

TINA

The logo inside my down jacket claims beauty
is function. And a Ted Talk argues people find
open spaces with clumps of trees beautiful
because that's where humans first survived.
So just let the next apocalypse try
and wrangle our spring.

Here the plum stills a blizzard of petals
and hickories lift flame-shaped buds high.
Dead leaves fallen, sky blues all the way
down to the ground, baring the ridgeline
enough that we watch rain wash over
its hip, waist, breast.

That's the function, seeing what's coming
before it arrives. "If we can see it,"
is what I say, prompting you to call me
your "apocalyptical one," like you have
for forever. But don't you know, my love,
one sets two in motion.

Now you warn about bird flu swooping in,
markets crashing. You say we'll hole up here.
We're built for hard times. I say look
how spring functions, flexes. Watch
those daffodils pick themselves up
after rain, see how they leave sun
trying to match their brilliance.

Coping Mechanisms JIM

Back in the fall we were so damn parched, every day was about the want for water. My neighbor, Nick—the one who's good to us, to everyone here, and who gave me divining rods, showed me how to dowse—he could not find his bearings. Everything had lost its sense.

"It's all dying," he called me on the phone to say as if Tina's talk of the apocalypse had claimed him. "I don't know what to do."

Well into spring now, the rains bring flash floods, and every night lightning strikes like a blue match across the skylight. I worry Hydrangea will be a field of splinters and pine needles come morning, but seldom what I fear happens the way I expect.

Everything is blooming except the sides of dogwoods that took on stroke during the drought—their shallow roots could not find enough water. Neither could the poplars. The first to shoot up from the ground, they are the first to die.

So I go out looking for them, standing dead trees that can be left to cure until I have time to make them into legs and rafters. And I watch for the late blooming maples and sourwoods to green, to prove they've lasted.

Tina and I got through the drought with an AC box on full blast, with toe-dips in Sally Branch, peanuts and beer when it was too hot to cook, bourbon and ice on the deck when we needed to repair our relationship with the stars.

"We'll go for a drive," I said to Nick after a month of his calls. I was on the deck, looking at the haze, the leaves wilting and palish. "Get you a beer. Get you out of your home. Somewhere, anywhere, just tell me where you want to go."

The phone got quiet, and if I'd been paying attention, I would've heard the dogwoods and poplars dig their roots in, ready to welcome any storm.

Tight Gradient

JIM

In that moment, poplars split along drought-sores, chestnut oaks
snapped from their bogged-in roots, and we held our breath afraid
every tree would fall. Just before, we had watched, waited for the
line of storms to reach the woods. It was what the weather authority
promised, "a tight gradient," as if the wind was being pushed through
a pinhole at us. We held our breath not thinking, not moving in the
center of our home, protected—hoping for that—though glass walls
are an awful thin buttress. Truth is we were held by the grace of trees
bending into their neighbors' branches.

Sixteen Fibs I Like Telling Myself

1. What the poster at the rest area said is true: *Alabama is America's Amazon.*

2. Turkey Creek's vermillion darter is the macaw of fish, though it is much rarer.

3. Rarer is better.

4. Seeing the vermillion darter is my birthright since Dad and his sisters tubed Turkey Creek's sandstone slides.

5. Standing waist-deep and gazing through my shadow I see one.

6. Blue-finned, silver-scaled, he puckers up, kisses my sandal, makes me blush.

7. His kisses mean he loves me.

8. The Peruvian Amazon, humidity and foliage thick, smacked of sweet home the moment I arrived.

9. Seeing macaws, morpho butterflies, tapirs, pink dolphins, and monkeys was easy, commonplace.

10. But I would have traded seeing them all for a glimpse of a poison arrow frog, the rarest Amazonian creature.

11. I can recognize bluegill, Alabama's most common fish by how they peck at my legs for salt.

12. This isn't one of them.

13. Right and wrong can sort themselves out.

14. Vermillion doesn't mean red. It means blue or teal, the color of his gorgeous fins.

15. If I part these waters and let awe pass un-dampened, the
    vermillion darters, the poison arrow frogs, all the rare
    creatures common to this and that Amazon will be saved.

16. I'm bound to see them all.

Hold Still

Puddles around here dry up
too quick for tadpoles to frog and toad.
My casserole dishes hold
only so much rain, never enough
tadpoles to keep the choir
crooning. Once a whippoorwill
blued our nights, a call so anxious
we joked he couldn't get any.
Or enough. Like the Bob White
I whistled to as a kid, he's gone.
I'm trying, but I'm no good
at being a puddle. Or knowing
how fast Thwaites may melt.
But I get how hard it is to hold
and hold still, to be sucked at
from below and above, to be overflown,
to keep edges gradual.
I want tadpoles to taste land
and return. And bees to wade in
and take a sip without drowning.
But it's hard to keep clean
and remain dirty enough
for mosquitoes, dragonflies,
and toads, to be both
watering hole and open womb.

Drought Song

JIM

"The big pines are dying," Pop tells me on the phone. For a hundred years they've cooled his house with their longleaf branches, kept their own stars and pulled the sky into place.

Nick has fingers crossed. He hopes some plants in his garden—"all that time spent and money"—trick death into bloom come spring.

Right now mountain fires around Augusta are bruising the horizon.

Water restrictions in effect. No burning allowed.

Another neighbor's well went bust last week.

The local water authority says they've got plenty in underground tanks in reserve. I can still get water there.

The land is burning, and the cows on Pop's farm have been going through the bales. Not enough to last winter.

Many people have told me they've not seen this, nothing like this, so dry for so long, 62 days and counting.

The weather authority—we have so many authorities here—takes to his pulpit about a pattern flip, about future rain to believe in.

The red-tail wings off the powerline because she can't quit.

The bullfrogs and lizards dry up in the sand.

Last month when I was down visiting Pop, we walked past my brother's cotton field.

Defoliated, no storm to wash the chemicals into the dirt and out to the creeks, that cotton, like snow, is never going to melt.

What Bob Wills sang of, and Pop helped his mother pick, didn't matter if fingers got scratched raw until cut open.

Along the edge of the field, we tried not to breathe it in. We slipped into dust like it was water.

In Place

TINA

　　　　We pass through the grasp
and cling of briers,
　　　　under dogwoods opening
their white crosses,
　　　　to plant Ozark chinquapins,
hoping to bring them back
　　　　from blight.
I peer into each hole
　　　　we step over,
wondering who lives here,
　　　　whose neck bends,
whose legs curl,
　　　　who takes rest
in this womb of soil.
　　　　I want them for neighbors.
Am I some body
　　　　these tree roots yawn for?
Can I take shelter
　　　　in their place?

TABLE OF OUR ROUTINE

Say we spend our last moments staring
at each other, hands knotted together,
clutching the dog, watching the sky burn.
Say, It doesn't matter. Say, That would be
enough. Say you'd want this: us alive,
right here, feeling lucky.

— ADA LIMÓN

Refuge

This is how we settle into luck—a short road trip so we can sit across a windrow of trees, a pavilion roped off with *Keep Out*, and a marshy lake knotted with cranes, gossipy and whooping.

Alabama is where they winter, where they call each other with the same ancient pitch my aunts used when asking about family while peeling back plastic wrap and tinfoil, mapping out reunion casseroles on a long table.

You have their declarative hands, able to maneuver cheese wedges alongside apple slices on the board our termite guy cut from walnut.

I open wine we got at the S & S because you forgot a bottle from home. "I thought I had everything," you say, then words lose their voice to our ritual on this bench we like at Wheeler.

The sun fattens the horizon into a red sea the lake had been once, and my hands turn cold—I forgot my gloves. You forgot yours, too.

Bread becomes tasteless except for its spongy texture. Wine turns into ice water. Or maybe it's the chill in my bones, on my tongue. Doesn't matter. We would stay forever if they left the gates open.

The sandhill cranes start to fly off to roost in the cornstalks and trees. They chatter with sea-light on their bellies, raft after longneck raft, hitching grooves into the sky.

"Look," you say, pointing above my head, but that raft of birds is gone by the time I've turned, trying not to miss what you find beautiful.

Why I seek to know myself in your love I don't understand. But I see the cranes now that we are in bed in our loft, how half their body was dark in shadow and the other half visible,

the same divide as where your grandmother's quilt of octagons ends and your round shoulders begin, white feathers coppered like the full moon's penny above the skylight I built.

So you could see out, I set a piece of glass across this wooden box.

Not Gone Away

Maybe it's all bee swarm now,
      how I can stand inside
their swirl, opening my arms
      to their thrum as I once did
to thunder and lightning blown
      across river. Yes, I still want
to swell like Jon Baptiste
      crowing "Oooo-wee,"

but I doubt I'll scale Royal Arches
      again. And the rapids
I once surfed now keep me holding
      my own beer. Only my dog
runs hard after glints of light
      or shadows of soaring
hawks. She tears off as if to burst
      her heart and hurtle
herself faster than time.

It was, for sure, a thrill chasing
      the eclipse to Tennessee,
you, me, and our dog lying down
      on a blanket in the sun,
then quicksilver light that wasn't
      light. The sky dropped
its blue and we were just gone
      so tipsy with shadow. It's that.
And the woozy of the subfloor
      of our cabin, calling us
to step, turn, take time to sway,
      like we always do
when we hear Sly sing,
      "I Want to Take You Higher."

Ease

We are old hands at love, having learned how to steer the wind
around the windrow, pluck splinters from the heart. On our ten acres,
shooting stars reside in cedars with chickadees and wrens so that we
might gather their branch-light for use. On Sundays, our church is
dancing on a subfloor that needs a proper floor over it. "Someday," you
say, "we will manage each other's counterstep by dovetailing hands
in pocket." We will split the earth and fill it with stars and seeds.
When we listen to Sally Branch run after a storm, we joke that she has
become a horse we should run after. But until we catch her, you cut
rosemary for supper. I fix shelves to hold whatever you need. We sit at
the table of our routine.

Nothing Else

TINA

When the soup's on and in
the bowl. When all is salted,
    warmed, when bread
melts butter. When the table's set,
    and nothing else is wanted
but what is within reach.
    A grind of pepper, your knee.
My body shifts into savoring,

    and the nestling's wings
carry it to the next branch.
    Where clouds unlace, unraveling
into jeans turned cut-offs,
    then the sun snaps wide
its cleanest sheets.

Sunday, Now Our Day

TINA

of crepes and dancing to wwoz.
        Of sunlight breaking
through and hummingbird squabbles.
        The mimosas are good,
not too much OJ. The dancing is better,
        it makes me woozy with love.
How our home perches on this ridge,
        a draft could lift us
into turning like turkey vultures.
        They are beautiful from afar
and like Skeksis up close.
        One at the corvid center
wanted to untie my laces,
        her pink shins reminded me
of faded long-handles.
        She stepped toward me
as elegant as any bird
        tilting their head.

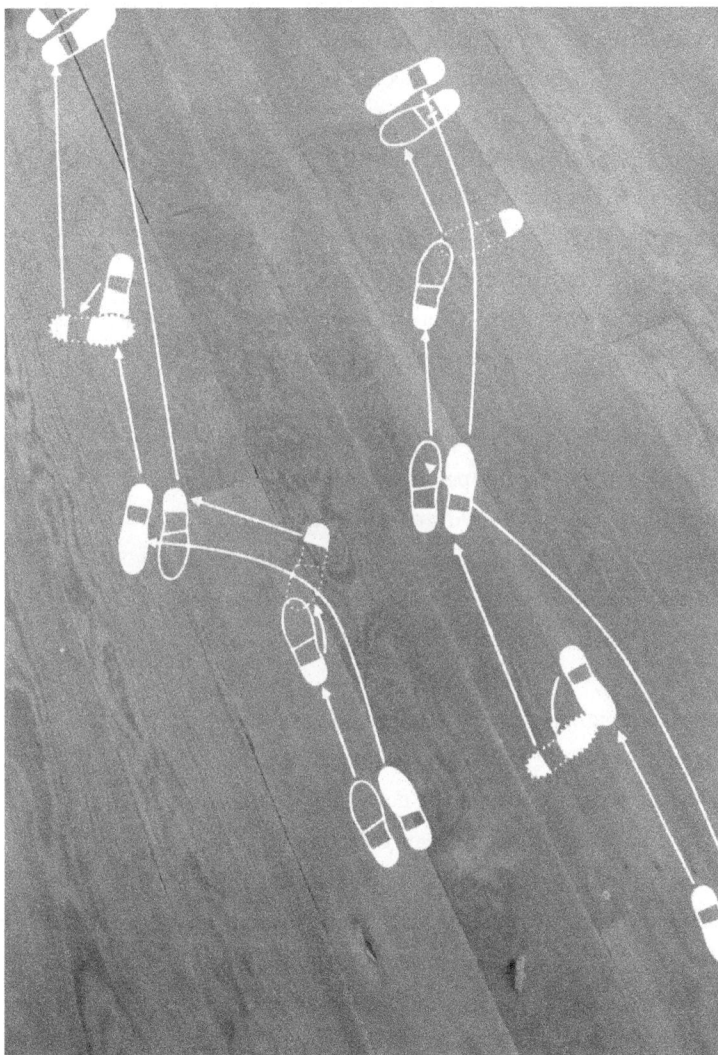

Odds Are

We have been betting on nobody but us
moving out here, betting hunters would go
on bagging bucks and leasing acreage,
betting nobody rich enough to dig a well
would want to drive a rutted road past
rusted semis and trailers. We bet on cedars
thickening into ramparts around our glass
walls, thwarting everybody from our sleeping
beauty. Odds are against us winning the lottery.

Friends said it's easier to get struck by lightning,
claimed only the poor get duped by somebody winning.
Like capitalism I thought but didn't say or admit
we're poor enough to sometimes bet our ages plus the date
we met will win us a year living in the French Quarter,
a new truck, and a restaurant for my brother.

But now new neighbors push through the cedars and gouge
the ridge here to move dirt there, we bet more often,
trying to win what we have right now. Odds are against
that pair of bald eagles gliding over to survey
the ridge will nest in our pines, against trillium
remaining untrampled, against Sally Branch sallying
forth forever. Ain't that America for you and me?
Where winning means buying it all, gating it off,
keeping this wild slumber to oneself? That's the dream,
to be the valiant one. Nothing like those people.

Where We Live Is Who We Are

*The Romans read places like faces, as outward
revelations of living inner spirit.*
— CHARLES W. MOORE ET AL.

The dog whimpers at the door, so I come down from the sleeping loft to
unlatch the lock. She bolts into the open without a kiss. Out west the
moon nestles where the sun will set over Cherty Ridge this evening.
But right now, the sun is throwing a pink curtain for the dog to run
through. If she jumps out of her mind and bites the moon—she's done
it before—I'll have to get my coat and hat, call her down. And if she
does not fall to me, I'll have to climb the ladder she made out of cedar
branches, retrieve her like I did my daughter who wouldn't let go the
top of a tall holly once. She was four. The dog is nine. I can no longer
reason love. But I don't want you to wake up to worry.

Before dawn, a star spun through the skylight to soothe my ear's
tuning fork ache. When that burst of light ended, your first car—a
green Dodge Dart Swinger—raced up from the bottom of our ridge
alongside hooves stabbing the earth. Then the car swerved, vanishing
with the deer into the trees.

Last night, the ridge became a humpbacked whale with the moon out,
with all those spiny hawthorns on its porcupine back. This was before
I climbed the ladder to our loft bed, before the star spun ear bones into
light, before the hooves and the Dart. I looked but could not find the
possum tail of ridge, though I have walked down and found the spring
under its belly. You sloshed tadpoles into the spring's clear water in
October to make them into winter pollywogs. "Survive," all that you
whispered.

Chigger Braille

You call your skin chigger braille because all the bites you got in the
garden, because a snake was coiled around a rabbit, and that baby's cry
brought you into the meadow in your long summer dress the chiggers
like to cling to.

Now, days later, you can't help but scratch, worried about impetigo you
fear. But the chigger braille along your spine you can't reach. Those
are the banished stars from your milky way, puckered into dewy, waxy
red bites.

Oh, my love, let me touch you there. What irritates you most, I desire.
You should slap my face for thinking such. You should remind me of
the rules of love—"Scratch if you want, please, but don't desire what
itches me." So I will keep quiet the words I find on your back made by
insects skin-hungry-drunk, looking for place to burrow into home.

Gain the Ocean

TINA

So chubby, that chuckle
    of a turkey filtering
through the wood, wooing
    thunder's grumble
to come hither and soak
    clothes drying on the line.
"Never mind," you say,
    "Here it only circles.
Storm or drizzle rarely comes
    round." But it's rousing,
that turkey flaunting how he's floof,
    saying he is fan and featherbed
and all the fun ever—
    he's ever what you need.
I kiss the back
    of your neck and whisper,
"Come on, old gobbler, let's
    rain until rain's done."

If You, Then Me

TINA

If you are bluestem,
       I am fire pink.
If you are deck chair,
       I am hammock.
If you are coffee brewed
       into a perfect cup,
I am your banana bread sidekick.
       If you are "Give Him Cornbread,"
I am "Lovely Day."
       If you are hawk etching
awe into sky, I am tadpole
       swishing puddle wonder.
Yes, you foot shuffle
       while I eye roll.
And you wrap up in flannel sheet
       beside my silk pillow case.
You are forever Cades Cove
       while I am always Coosa River.
For a decade, you've been fungi
       alongside my algae,
meaning we're lichen,
       we love and like
so symbiotically,
       we bloom as one.

An Early Snow JIM

When we walked out with the dog, she sniffed around like the snow would do her harm. Then up the road, she dove into broom sedge to see what could happen. Black fur and brown sedge tangled, a thick-furred rabbit hightailed it out. At the tree line, branches held up clump after clump of white, and the dog, no longer a dog, leaped like deer. We kept walking, our faces heated to a blush. Far off, she kept barking. When I saw you smiling, I realized I was doing the same, that this is what happens after the world you think you know reveals itself to be something more.

GLOSSARY

2×6 or 2×4 — These are tricky terms. These boards are not 2 inches by 6 inches or 2 inches by 4 inches, but generally are more like 1¾ by 5¾ or 1¾ by 3¾, which is totally misleading. I have a vague memory of announcing with great cockiness that I could measure two inches or four by dimensions of a 2×4. While I don't remember the specifics of that situation, I still feel the sting of my arrogance as much as my ignorance. But it taught me that a 2×4 is the dimensions of a board when it is rough sawn (like our cedar beams that hold up the loft are literally 4 by 6 inches). Once they are planed to make them smooth, they end up a quarter to half inch shorter, thinner, less. I like that it asks me to keep in mind and appreciate the work that came before: the felling of trees, the rough cut of the saw mill, the planing that smooths boards down. That wins me over, just a little. (TINA)

Ada and Dail — Ada says, "I love your home as much as mine." And for good reason. Their home on St. George Island is made of glass and wood with the same open design, though their view is of pelicans and the bay. I looked at how their home was put together to figure out how to build the glass cabin (Pop's house was my other home-of-reference). Dail passed in 2016. He had great comedic timing. He knew when to give a punchline in silences, and I keep listening for his gruff voice when things get quiet. Ada's routine? Take care of all the animals on the island—birds, cats, raccoons,

squirrels, and turtles—just as she takes good care of us. She was a teacher. So was Dail. She's an editor, a writer, the founder of the University Honors Program at UAB, and she spent a lot of years living in cities. But once she started living surrounded by nature, she found where she wants to be. (JIM)

Aunt Trish and Uncle Gene — gave us old windows, quilts my Grandmother (Uncle Gene's sister) made, almost all the Christmas decorations we own, more things and love than I can measure. When I gave them a copy of my chapbook, Uncle Gene gave me a compliment I treasure. "Now this, this takes a mind." (TINA)

Architect/Dylan — A couple of years after helping build the cabin's bones, Dylan applied to Auburn's architecture program. The first night of summer classes when he called he said, "I started at seven this morning, just got done. God I love it, Pop-pop. I love it so much." His voice was the happiest I'd heard.

"Don't forget this," I said. I knew what this meant for him. When your kid finds what matters but he can't fully name yet, you feel.

For a semester, he worked and took classes at the Rural Studio.

Sometimes in a store people will say Dylan and I are brothers and those are the days I feel young. But his hair is thicker, redder, his beard longer. He's lankier.

And he's now an architect in B town—an unexpected outcome of building the glass cabin. (JIM)

Broom Sedge — pronounced broom sage around here, is what we call bluestem or anything that looks like what I once imagined wheat to look like, brown, tall, twisting stalks. I called it wheat as a kid. It grows in the sunlit places, fields and margins and disturbed land. And yes, brooms can be made of it, something we have yet to try. Best of all, it provides habitat for rabbits and birds. (TINA)

Buckets — are essential to our life in the cabin in three ways: 1) we snap a toilet seat on one and use it as THE bucket as in THE John, 2) Jim sets one under our sink to catch all the gray water, 3) and we leave buckets on our deck to catch rain water, aka laundry water, that falls off our roof. Either LET'S DO THIS or DO IT RIGHT is printed on the side of these blue and orange buckets, which is either odd or encouraging. (TINA)

Butterflies — from posting pictures of these visitors on Facebook— which I couldn't resist because how often do you get to hold a butterfly in your hands?—I learned from Randy Blythe that most of our butterflies are spicebush swallowtail, which are velvety black-blue with a distinctive tail on each wing. There are a few yellow butterflies that are eastern swallowtails, but they didn't get caught in our windows as often as the spicebushes did. (TINA)

Clerestory — Wouldn't it be cool if clerestory were spelled clearstory, as in it makes the story clear? As I type that I like the idea "restory" part of the word as if it tells our story better and again. A clerestory is a row of windows just under the eaves. I spent weeks climbing our scaffolding to create frames and then framing the panes. In our case the tops are cut at an angle to follow the two-foot difference between the wall height on the east wall (tallest side, so tall Jim had to frame the panes closest to this side) and the west wall (the shortest). Mornings we wake in our loft bed, these panes are eye-level, each framing tree trunks and limbs. (TINA)

Dave — as in Dave McRae or Dirty Dave who designs, sews, and sells kneepads and other caving gear and apparel at caving events and is one of the finest cavers and friends I know. He is as generous as he is brilliant at figuring out how to make things from fabric, wood, metal, etc. (TINA)

Ginny — was the first neighbor I met out here. She worked all week, but on weekends she walked the dirt road. Ginny had a dog, Gizmo, that would take our gallon jugs we filled with water to help dig holes for the foundation. *Who's stealing our milk jugs?* we wondered. Ginny said, "I come home and there are these jugs in the driveway. I'm sorry—they're useless. He's chewed the handles up pretty bad." I told her not to worry about it, those jugs had many uses—holding milk, carrying water, and entertaining a charming dog. The road is a lot emptier when we go walking since she passed. (JIM)

H — When H came home to Pitts, Georgia, in the 1950s, my grandfather hired him to be a tractor driver and let him live in a tenant farmhouse built at the turn of the century. H didn't own a car, didn't like to walk, and didn't like to make his own breakfast, so he drove the tractor, which my grandfather let him keep in the yard, the mile and a half to town to eat before turning rows. Everyone started calling the place H's house for he was the last tenant to live there. It is the first marker brought up in any discussion of the map of farms north of town. H's house passed hands to my uncle and then to his son, Wayne, and when I told Pop I needed floorboards for the glass cabin, he immediately thought of the tongue and groove heart pine in H's. Wayne lives out in LA. His only connection to where he grew up is his monthly phone conversations with my father. Though it is often stated otherwise, the truth is nothing gets done without talking first. Pop made the call to Wayne who said, yes, I could have the boards, who said that really, he wanted the place torn down. But if you drive the Vienna Highway from I-75 to Pitts, H's house is still there grown up in dog fennel, still holding on. (JIM)

Hatches — are what we call anywhere where we put in hinges so part of the wall can open to let air in. There are eight 6"x24" hatches just under the eaves. Four on each side. They were a total pain to put in because they are so much work. First, the screens had to be made and put in. Then the door portion had to be cut and sanded down to fit. And then we had to check that they would hinge fully open. And each one takes two hinges that required three screws each and a handle, which we pull open with a long stick or rod. It took Jim the same amount of time to put four tiny little hatches in on the east wall while I did all the clerestory windows on the north wall and that's not counting the time it took for all the west wall hatches. (TINA)

High Life — the cheap beer, that is, the champagne of beers. An essential way to unwind after a long day of cabin building, but also a marker between busting our asses building and taking a moment to savor that we're done, if only for the day. (TINA)

Jeff and Nancy — showed up when help was needed most. I'd never built a house before, but they had—a strawbale house I'd visited and talked with them about. After Dylan and I braced the walls of the cabin, they showed up with ladders and tools to help put the rafters in place because while you can get away with a lot of imprecise construction, it's important to get the bones of the roof right. Most days that winter, there was ice on the subfloor and us heading up the ladders with boards and drills. Maybe because I'm tall, I'm not good on ladders —I don't have faith in my balance —but Jeff would climb to the very top rung and do a 360 as if he was born a squirrel. (JIM)

Jessi — I first met my daughter Jessi when writing a story in a college computer lab. This was back when typed-in words showed up orange on a black screen, the monitor as big as a block of ice. I heard a voice, turned, and right there was the beautiful face of one-year-old Jessi, her mother holding her up. I always say the bond between us is so strong because we chose each other that day and still do. Jessi was and is the best bicycle rider in the world (once she got old enough to start riding). And though not a housebuilder yet, she was inspired by what we did and now knows her way around a miter saw and drill, having built furniture for her home. (JIM)

Madi — "She's a jewel," Pop said after Madi, Dylan, and I put up a new fence for him. I couldn't agree more. The thing about work, you don't know if someone will last until they get into it. When I worked the melon fields in high school, took only walking a few rows in the sun before some had to step away and go home. But when we made that fence for Pop, Madi had no let up. She got down in the gnats to set the barbed wire. She slammed in the T-posts. She took breaks only when I told

her she had to. When she helped build the cabin, it was the same. Her boyfriend at the time kept trying to tell Madi how to dig the holes for the foundation. This was May, hot and humid, and he was worrying her like those gnats. Madi said, "You worry about your own damn hole." And he left her alone after that. (JIM)

Money (or the lack thereof) — It took two years before Tina returned from Oregon and we moved into our cabin. During that time Dylan and I lived in my apartment in B town, and we drove out to Hydrangea Ridge to build when we could. Because I couldn't buy on my own what I needed, I leaned on Pop's home improvement cards for lumber and supplies. And I had to lean on Dylan for labor I couldn't pay upfront. The best I could do for him was provide food, shelter, a little spending cash.

Every time I wrote out the rent check, I felt kicked in the gut. $1000 poorer the first of the month. $12,000 gone every year into an air-conditioned office, where the person behind the desk was too busy checking out their phone to even look up and acknowledge what I was giving. Not their dollars lost, I guess.

Dylan helped me dig holes for the foundation, lift walls into place, even nail the ceiling boards down after his wrists ached with tendonitis. He kept up with his hours, and once Tina and I moved out to Hydrangea, I wrote Dylan a check the first of the month, half what I'd been paying on rent. The other half went to Pop toward the debt I owed him.

I wanted to be able to say, "Anyone can do what I'm doing without help." But that's a myth. Even the money here is secondhand. (JIM)

Nail Apron — a tie-on pocket for nails, screws, and even some lip balm. Made of cotton, they come for cheap or free according to where you buy your building supplies. I like them much better than a tool belt, which looks badass because it is leather but it's too bulky and heavy for me to work in. Jim, on the other hand, loves a tool belt. (TINA)

Neighbors — in addition to Nick and Judy, include Mac who gave us our mailbox, scrapes the dirt roads until ruts are passable if not gone, and is the person who would give you the shirt off his back. And Peggy and Sue, aka "the ladies" who've lived on our ridge the longest, started out like us, living for years without running water, love to tell jokes and laugh. They share my concern for tadpoles and created a sign they placed beside the puddle that read, "Frog pond. Let them live. Drive around." Nina, our newest and youngest neighbor, a climate activist, who lives in a wall tent she erected while she builds an off-grid tiny house. She gives us hope for the future, and her charming dog makes us laugh. We also count: pack rats gathering hickory nuts under the hood of the van and under the deck, the wrens and swifts nesting in our eaves, the anoles and skinks skittering over the deck, the praying mantises and walking sticks pacing our windows and screens, obviously toads and frogs, the pileated woodpeckers, the barred owls, salamanders we feel fortunate to encounter, and even the timber rattlers who according to Nick and Judy like to do it in the road, twining around one another so they stand a couple feet high. (TINA)

Laura Ingalls — the author whose books I checked out from the library and read over and over, the character on *Little House on the Prairie* I watched closely, the girl I pretended to be when I braided my hair, when I didn't let wearing a dress or being a girl stop me from running through fields, damming up streams, climbing trees with a Laura Ingalls book to read. (TINA)

Ozark Chinquapin — a smaller variety of American Chestnut that we are trying to propagate on the ridge thanks to the efforts of The Ozark Chinquapin Foundation that locates and hand pollinates surviving Ozark chinquapins in order to restore their native forests with what they hope will be blight resistant trees. For a $30 donation, the Foundation mails us 5 or 6 seedlings to plant and, fingers-crossed, aid their efforts. This is more affordable than spending $300 on a hybrid of an American and Chinese Chestnut trees. (TINA)

Ride 'em Radiators — this was what Jim and I would call out to each other when we used the very first "heating system" of the cabin —plug-in, oil filled radiators. A single radiator had heated my above-garage apartment in Oregon, but two radiators were no match for our high ceilings and walls, parts of which were "dried-in" with mere sheets of visqueen. So we took to straddling them to keep warm and hollering out "ride 'em radiators" until we were able to set up Vestal for heating the cabin. (TINA)

Rural Studio — founded by Samuel Mockabee in the early 1990s, this architecture program allows students from Auburn University to design and build for communities in West Alabama. The first buildings completed came from found materials. More recent projects include customized $20,000 homes, a fire station, and library. The first time I heard of the Rural Studio I expressed an interest in architecture to my undergraduate advisor in Intercultural Studies at the University of Montevallo, Mrs. Blackmon, who told me to take enough science and math and I could transfer to Auburn and build fun things with Mockabee. When chemistry proved to be too much, I stayed at Montevallo and earned a B.A. instead of a B.S., and delayed building fun for two decades. (TINA)

Sawdust — is without a doubt my nemesis, the entity that I hate most, something I battle constantly. I cut a board and I'm sprayed with sawdust. Kneel or sit or lie down on the floor, I'm covered in sawdust. And this is the thing, sawdust is splinters ground up. And all splinters find ways to dig into skin. Jim, who believed until I set him straight that if you leave a splinter in your skin it would work its way into a vein and then on to your heart where it would kill you, acts like sawdust is fine, as if sawdust is easy as dirt. But that's ridiculous. Dirt washes away or turns into mud. Sawdust is always looking for a way to stick me, literally. (TINA)

Scaffolding — one of the many things that Jim's Dad, aka Pops D, aka the Great Dr. Delano Roosevelt Braziel, procured from somebody in South Georgia to help us build the cabin. Having built his own home he knew what we needed. Standing about six foot tall, it looks like a gray stage set on top of two metal ladders on wheels that hold a shelf beneath the stage. The stage is 2'x8' with plenty of room to maneuver while framing windows and to hold the many window-framing accoutrements. If someone made an action figure of me, a Barbie of window framing, I'd come with a nail apron, a silicone gun, a hammer, boards, panes of glass, and scaffolding. (TINA)

Shellac/Shellacking — we used polyurethane aka poly to seal the boards, but shellac/shellacking rolls off the tongue better, speaks a bit to the situation I found myself in specifically. As in:

Poor Tina, she lacks
a home so she shellacs
the boards she likes
to build what she'd
otherwise lack. (TINA)

Silicone — aka "silly cone" or
"sill a cone," all appropriate
ways to refer to the glue-like
substance that squirts out of the
caulk gun and drips out of it and
stains anything it touches with a
glop of resin that hardens. Surely
this isn't the stuff fake boobs
are made of—that would be a silly
cone, indeed. (TINA)

Stringers — the diagonal boards
that hold each tread of a stair.
We used pre-cut stringers for the
steps to our front door which
made building them much easier
than the loft stairs. (TINA)

Swap Shop — a local radio show
that announces things people want
to buy or sell via sharing phone
numbers for buyers and sellers.
How such a show still exists in
the time of the internet, I have
no idea, but I'm grateful for the
entertainment of imagining people
out there, pencil in hand, waiting
to jot down the digits for a
used lawn mower. Dylan, Jim, and
I nearly peed ourselves laughing
when a woman called in saying she
needed a window unit, a drill, and
a male guinea pig. (TINA)

Tarrant — The second time I drove
out divining for land, I took the
State 79 spur off the interstate
and wound up in the city of
Tarrant. A lot of stoplights in
Tarrant, which gave me time to
take notice of the many factories

and power lines, used car
dealerships, more check-cashing
places than I've ever seen, and at
the center, a flame that shoots
out of a pipe from the ABC Coke
plant.

Little did I know I'd be driving
back and forth through Tarrant to
build the cabin. I still make the
same trek when I leave Hydrangea
Ridge to work in B town. That
flame marks my journey, and
I've gotten to know it for the
pollution it emits burning coal
into coke down in its ovens. At
times the flame burns so high, it
is mesmerizing, beautiful.

The symbol for B town is Vulcan,
the god of fire and forge. A
statue of Vulcan sits atop Red
Mountain overlooking B town with
an iron spear point in his hand
instead of a lit torch. To find
that torch, you have to drive
through the city of Tarrant. (JIM)

Toenailing — technically means to
drive in a nail at an angle. But
for us, it also means working with
your loved ones as demonstrated
by Jim or Dylan or me breaking
out into song, "Toe-nailing with
my baby," the theme song of our
glass cabin building. (TINA)

Tom — in addition to building
his own cabin, taught solar-
panel installation at the local
community college and ran a solar-
panel installation business. He
and his real estate agent wife,
Sue, kept bees and tended a
garden, invited everyone in our
Oregon neighborhood over to carve
pumpkins for Halloween. That's how

I met them. After that, they were always helping me out, offering tomatoes from their garden, showing me their bee swarms, giving me a lift to get my van fixed. When Tom grew more medical marijuana than he needed, I found grad students willing to take the excess off his hands for a fee. (TINA)

Traci — aka Scout (after Harper Lee's lead character in *To Kill a Mockingbird*) and I began trading books and taking hikes together once we met in our high school typing class. I quickly became friends with her whole family. When liquidating her landscaping business, she gave us a rain barrel and tarps and all manner of plants. The very best gift she gave us was the starving cat that wrapped his legs around her leg outside her parent's trailer. Though her husband was allergic, she took that cat home, nursed him back to health, and gave him to us. We renamed him Satchmo, beginning our tradition of jazz cats. (TINA)

The Cat — we have now is Mose, who thinks he is the king of the cabin and therefore he is. As a kitten he was thrown into a Baton Rouge dumpster where he was rescued by Madi who gave him to us. He's a gorgeous gray stripes, green eyes, pink nose. We often wonder who would throw such beauty and royalty away. (TINA)

The Dog — we "inherited" from Dylan. He named her Patience, but that proved to be too aspirational for a dog with such energy. So we

renamed her Pbutt and sometimes call her "the butt." She loves to walk, fetch balls, and wedge herself between us on the couch. When we dance, she leaps around and barks a bit trying to figure out how to join us. (TINA)

Tread — the horizontal board placed on the stringers that you step on to climb a stair. Each step in a stair is another tread. (TINA)

Turkey Vultures — I first recognized their beauty while climbing at Mount Cheaha. I was belaying atop a cliff where a bird would swerve, swoop, and swing around so graceful I wondered if it were something other than a vulture. In Oregon, I visited a corvid sanctuary in Eugene and met a wonderful turkey vulture who in the wild had taken to approaching people, particularly women and children, and untying their shoes. Close up and caged, the regal glide wasn't there, but I was still taken by her pink legs and head, how she came close, how I could see through her nostrils. I love how they patrol our skies and grounds. (TINA)

Vestal — yes, as in virgin or as in the woodstove manufacturer circa 1970s that forged this iron behemoth and decked her out with flames and the name vestal across her doors. Those flames are fitting for how warm, at times even too warm, she keeps the cabin. During our first winter, when the Snowpocalypse took out power across the state and stopped traffic on surface

roads and I-65, leaving commuters
stranded in their vehicles
overnight, we had no trouble.
Vestal kept us cozy. We were even
able to heat water for coffee,
make pancakes and soup on her
flattop. (TINA)

Visqueen — large rolls of thick,
opaque, plastic sheeting that I
first encountered when I worked
as a wilderness counselor. At the
wilderness program we used copious
rolls of it as walls for the
"tents" we constructed out of logs
and tarps. (TINA)

ACKNOWLEDGMENTS

THANK YOU to the editors of the following publications where these poems and essays first appeared.

Exit 7	"Sixteen Fibs I Like Telling Myself"
High Horse Magazine	"September Prayer" and "Turkey Vultures"
Hobo Camp Review	"Without Varnish" and "Sunday, Now Our Day"
The New York Times	"What the Wind Carried Away"
POETRY	"Dandelion" and "Ephemeral Pool"
Poetry Birmingham	"Lay at My Feet"
Poetry Northwest	"Spontaneous Combustion"
Spittoon	"Become Kindling"
SWWIM	"The Flowering Pear" and "In Place"
Rooted by Thirst (Porkbelly)	"Hatches" and an earlier version of "First Winter, the Cabin"
What Things Cost (U of Kentucky)	excerpts from "Necessary Weight, Necessary Time"
Zone 3	excerpts from "Sally Branch"

The epigraph for "Strike It" comes from Ashley M. Jones's poem "In Blount County" that appears in *Magic City Gospel*. "Say Uncle" also refers to this poem.

"Honeymoon at Tor House" uses phrases from the poems by Robinson Jeffers that were read to us at Tor House.

"Least I'm Not as Picky as a Carolina Wren" quotes the penultimate line of Larry Levis's "Sleeping Lioness."

"Shadows Now" refers to Henri Cole's description of a praying mantis in his "Pillow Case with Praying Mantis."

The epigraph for "The Apocalypse" comes from Richard Hugo's poem, "Ovando," from his book, *The Lady in Kicking Horse Reservoir.*

"Table of Our Routine" quotes Ada Limón's "The Conditional" from her collection *Bright Dead Things.*

"Gain the Ocean" makes use of a phrase from Rumi.

We're forever grateful to Pop (Delano R Braziel) and Dylan for making our glass cabin life possible.

Thank you to our parents for their love.

We also want to thank Preston Browning for hosting us at his Wellspring House, and Ada Long for her editing acumen and just plain inspiration.

And thank you, Lauren Goodwin Slaughter aka "The Franchise," for connecting us to Pulley Press; Jessica Geil and Prakash Younger, for your suggestions on our book proposal; Wendy Reed, for the many carrots; Gillian Kimmel, for your notes on an early version of this book; Nicole Pomeroy, for your suggestions and proofreading; Russell Hehn and Gale Boyer, for promoting *Glass Cabin*; Kerry Madden, Julia Kolchinsky Dasbach, Regan Huff, Chloe Martinez, Luisa Caycedo-Kimura, Aaron Caycedo-Kimura, Mandy Gutmann-Gonzalez, and to Lauren and Wendy again for your feedback on poems and prose that appear here.

We thank Dan Shafer for the care you took in the design of this book; and Dylan Braziel for creating such a beautiful photo collage for the cover; thanks, Rebecca Gayle Howell, for your lovely introduction.

And thank you, Frances McCue and Greg Shaw, for celebrating rural poets and believing in our book. And thank you, Frances, for seeing things we couldn't, for helping us find *Glass Cabin*'s arc and shape, and, most of all, for your friendship. ◣

ALSO BY TINA MOZELLE BRAZIEL

Rooted by Thirst

Known by Salt

ALSO BY JAMES BRAZIEL

This Ditch-Walking Love

Snakeskin Road

Birmingham, 35 Miles